D1539915

THROUGH A
DAD'S EYES

THROUGH A DAD'S EYES

Searching for Answers, Finding God

TOMMY JONES

TATE PUBLISHING
AND ENTERPRISES, LLC

Through a Dad's Eyes
Copyright © 2014 by Tommy Jones. All rights reserved.

No part of this publication may be reproduced, stored in a retrieval system or transmitted in any way by any means, electronic, mechanical, photocopy, recording or otherwise without the prior permission of the author except as provided by USA copyright law.

Scripture quotations marked (NIV) are taken from the *Holy Bible, New International Version*®, NIV®. Copyright © 1973, 1978, 1984 by Biblica, Inc.™ Used by permission of Zondervan. All rights reserved worldwide. www.zondervan.com

The opinions expressed by the author are not necessarily those of Tate Publishing, LLC.

Published by Tate Publishing & Enterprises, LLC
127 E. Trade Center Terrace | Mustang, Oklahoma 73064 USA
1.888.361.9473 | www.tatepublishing.com

Tate Publishing is committed to excellence in the publishing industry. The company reflects the philosophy established by the founders, based on Psalm 68:11,
"The Lord gave the word and great was the company of those who published it."

Book design copyright © 2014 by Tate Publishing, LLC. All rights reserved.
Cover design by Rodrigo Adolfo
Interior design by Mary Jean Archival

Published in the United States of America
ISBN: 978-1-63122-137-8
Biography & Autobiography / Personal Memoirs
14.03.10

Dedication

To Brady, Will, and my loving wife, Beth. Together we have overcome. Together we are strong.

Acknowledgment

I would not have the courage to write this book if it wasn't for so many people who have shown they care, shown their support, and shown me God is good and at work. There are people who made me better along the way that don't even know they were involved.

First, I have to give the glory to God. Without his hand on my shoulder and without him showing me the way, I would not have the strength to write this story. It is with him I made it through writing these emotions and spending days and nights combating the tears as I recalled the last eight years and ponder the future.

I can't write this book and not thank the team of doctors and therapists who have cared for Brady over the years. From the first days until the last days of rehab, I am forever grateful for the will and determination you all showed, including the most recent doctors to work with him.

There is an endless amount of friends, coworkers, employers, and employees to thank for their help, kind words, meals, conversations, and leading me back to the

Lord. All of you know who you are, and I hope you now know how much I have cherished you over the years. Without you, who knows where I would be today.

Next, there isn't enough I can write or say to thank David and Barbara Jones, my loving parents. They have provided guidance and a shoulder to cry on when it was needed. I may not want to hear the things they say all the time, but which kid does? What I appreciate the most is the countless time they have given to me and my family during the last eight years—From coming to babysit our dogs, to the kids, and more recently, coming to help Beth take care of me when I was recovering from cancer surgery. Thanks for letting me lay in your lap to sleep, Dad, and thanks for the warm meals, Mom.

I am very lucky to have two moms and two dads. My in-laws are like my own parents, and I don't view them as in-laws like most. Larry and Mary Phillips have been there every step of this journey too. They have come for visits when we couldn't take it, taken the kids to their house so we could get a break, and even been there with a tissue for us. I pray I make them proud.

How do you thank someone who has taught you things they don't know about? My brother, Troy, didn't just recently help me find a love for golf and put up with my annoying swing, he has helped me get my mind off the reality of Brady when I needed it the most. I have another brother in Brad Phillips. Beth's brother and I seem to always laugh when we are together. It has been in those moments I found joy. Laughter is a great medicine, and everyone should laugh like we do when we get together, usually at someone else's expense, but nonetheless, we laugh.

Will Jones, my youngest son has worn many numbers during his young football career, but he will always be number one in my heart. He has overcome broken bones to a broken heart of letdown, and he continues to teach me that life is still life and each day is another day to look forward to. He has grown more in eight years than any other child I know while becoming the big brother when needed. He shows true love to his brother without ever questioning. This has taught him how to have kindness for others, though he may not know them.

To the inspiring Brady for allowing me to tell his story through my eyes. He has been through so much over the last eight years and has a long life ahead to be fulfilled with so many high points. He will graduate from high school soon, and the next phase of life will begin. Daddy will always be here for you no matter what.

Happy twentieth-year anniversary to my loving wife, Beth, who has stood by me through so much. From cross-country moves to a twenty plus-year career of changes, from waiting in the car at a meeting to waiting on me to get off the phone, you have given so much of your life for me. For all the nights you had to go to bed alone because I was traveling for work, I am sorry for the years I missed. You took care of me when I couldn't care for myself after surgery. You have been not only a caregiver but a giver of so much so I could chase my dreams and career, and I thank you. Without you, who knows what my life would be like, but I know one thing; it wouldn't be filled with the excitement I have today. I am amazed by your strength, your courage, and your love. God blessed me by having you as my wife. *I love you!*

Contents

Preface

As a parent, we never think that something rare and strange can happen to our kids. We are to protect and provide for our kids. We teach them about God, how life works and doesn't work, and what to do when faced with adversity.

I guess, growing up, I missed the lesson about being taught anything about adversity. Sure, I overcame family members passing away, my own failures, loss of friends, and everything else we go through in life as we grow up. But I never thought I would be standing where I am today. At times, I thank God; at times, I question him. Why? Why did he allow it to happen? I may never know the answer, but I continue to search for it.

Most of us, as parents, dream of the day our kid grows into a young adult, star athlete, successful career person, and the list goes on and on. For me, I dream of the day my son, Brady, can find peace with God's plan for him, and I pray for God to comfort him during his dark times.

As Brady continues to grow into an adult, his mother and I struggle to find the answers he deserves, find a way for him to live a life of normalcy, and prepare him for a life of dependency.

The winter of 2004, Brady had discovered snow skiing in Breckenridge, Colorado. The kid was quickly picking up all kinds of great sports as hobbies.

I was starting to schedule trips to the ER for broken bones, concrete road rash, and everything else kids tear up while riding bikes, skateboards, and skiing. Little did I know the upcoming trip to the ER would be for something nowhere related to sports, hobbies, or anything anyone would have predicted.

Life-altering events can be good or bad. What tough life-altering events have you faced? Have you overcome it, or did it engulf your soul, mind, and body? Mine took me by surprise and left me rather paralyzed for almost eight years. Years of rebellion, years of anger, and years of emptiness haven't been the answer either.

My life-altering event involves my oldest son and how I found myself years later. I hope my path to triumph gives you hope, motivation, and strength if you are struggling in life today.

I have never thought of myself as a writer or someone who could translate thoughts into a journal worth binding. After reflecting back on the last so many years, I felt led by God to share my story and to write as I have witnessed the time unfold.

Current Day

I am sitting at my newly constructed desk in my latest location of employment, my own study at home. I have soothing Christian music playing to keep me company as it turns 2:30 a.m. on July 28, 2013, fighting yawn after yawn to not throw in the towel and head downstairs for bed. I shouldn't be all that tired. I slept until almost 1:00 p.m. today. Of course, Buddy and Lucy, my goldendoodles, woke me up at 9:00 to go outside and eat breakfast. My day was pretty good, but it also involved a trip to the Ikea store. If anyone has ever been to one of those, you know that can turn out to be a three- to five-hour trip. I had to get my youngest son a new desk unit, then come home and build it. However, I have been very tired the last several months anyway. I have been keeping odd hours as I begin the next part of my life.

In May, after seven and a half years, I stepped away from a lucrative job to relax with my family. I haven't seen them much over that time period, considering I spent about 230 days traveling, so at forty-one, I thought it was time to come home. I am very blessed to have been given the opportunity and glad God gave me the way. Why did I do it? Life throws us curve balls, and I was thrown one bad pitch, so I came home.

When my wife and I sat down to discuss the opportunity, she was nervous and scared, but oddly enough, she was also encouraged and excited about it. As I sat with God for several mornings, I prayed his will be done and he lead me down the path for him. May 10 was my last day of employment. People have asked me, "What are you going to do?" I tell them, "I retired."

"At forty?" they typically reply. After I think about it, "Yes, at forty. God is good and knows what he is doing, so yes, at forty, I have retired." Sounds weird to say today. How did I do it? I have always told people, "If you can get $1,000,000 in the bank and $1,000,000 in mutual funds, then you could retire, pay off your mortgage, and relax. Or you could inherit the money or maybe write a bestselling novel or become a movie star."

Guess my book is done. I just gave you the answer on how to retire at forty. Thanks for reading. Just kidding. First of all, I didn't retire because I have $2,000,000 sitting around. My wife and kids wouldn't let me keep that kind of money—trust me. I also didn't recently inherit the money, unless someone hasn't told me yet. Bestselling novel? Considering this is my first book, I don't think that is it either. That only leaves becoming a movie star, but those who know me know I don't have the looks to be a movie star. For me, I guess none of those work.

My retirement is really a new beginning, but this time, with my family. I will be home more, like being retired, but I will be working on my own design firm. If the first ninety days is any sign of things to come, then maybe

I will be able to someday really retire and leave others in charge. But let me be very clear, this is all because of Jesus Christ and his power to open doors. I was at a local eatery last night with my wife Beth, and we were talking to a good friend of ours. I was telling her about my new beginning, and she said, "God opens doors, honey, and sometimes, he kicks us through them if we have been slow to see them in the past." She is so right.

Before May 10, 2013, I had no extra time to do anything to the point Beth made me hire a yard guy, so what time I might have to do things for her—I mean, with her—I could, maybe, get a hall pass from her to play golf with my buddies. I wanted to do this book, but before, I couldn't find the time or meet the people who could help me get it going. Since May 10, 2013, I have found time to do a few things around the house, launch a new firm, spend time with my kids, and take my wife on a date or two, and God has given me the time to focus on this book.

Why is this book so important to me? As you read it, you will uncover why, relive my emotions, hear pain in my words, laugh, and maybe cry. Well, I am not sure if there are many laughing points, but depending on your sense of humor, who knows.

Without hesitation, I give you my view through a dad's eye.

Memory Lane

B eth Phillips was this girl in my architectural design class in college. I had looked her way a few times but thought for sure she is way out of my league. She never talked to me or looked my way. She sat in the back of class, and I sat in the front. I was a nerd, and she liked to talk a lot to some guy who she knew. I think his mom might have taught her in high school or something. Oh, she likes to talk; did I mention that part?

The class was taught by an older guy by the name of Mr. Johnson. He was a nice guy and not too hard of a teacher. The class was really fun because we got to design and draw all the time. This class was like three hours long too, so there were plenty of breaks. I sat next to a guy I had met in another class. He carried a tackle box to the design class. After a few days of watching him, I went and bought one myself. Back then, the design class took so many drawing utensils, like architectural templates, lead, lead holder, scales, adjustable triangles, and many other things. The tackle box was the future architects' pocket protector. See, I was and am a nerd. If you carried a tackle box, people stared at you like you were a nerd. But things are looking up for those of us in the field of architecture. According to the July 2013 edition of British GQ, architects are rated number 5 on the "Ten Sexiest Jobs Ever."

One day during break, the guy who Beth always talked to said, "I bet you I can date her before you can." I just looked at him and replied, "Really? You are engaged, and I am not interested. She's too good for me." We went back and forth for a few minutes, and after him making several off-color remarks about Beth's backside, he said, "I bet fifty dollars."

Wait a minute, now there is money involved, I thought. "You will give me fifty dollars just to take her on a date? That's it?" He said, "Yep."

A few days later, on March 19, 1993—yes, I remember the date—I was at the mall with a friend. We walked by this store, and who did we see? There was Beth, working in a sunglass store. We walked in like we were interested in sunglasses. The next thing I knew, my so-called friend was asking her out for me. He asked her if she wanted to go to the circus that night. I didn't even know there was a circus in town. Beth looked right at me with a big smile and said, "You really will take me to the circus?" My response was like most twenty-year-olds', "Sure, if you want to go." She made a call because her grandparents were in town celebrating their fiftieth. After a few minutes, she said, "Okay, I can go. Pick me up here at nine."

After the circus and then midnight bowling, I took her to her car at about three thirty in the morning. I told her bye and that I had a nice time—you know, the usual thing you tell someone when the date was average. She

Through a Dad's Eyes

kind of followed suit with her departure, and off we went on our separate ways. No kiss, no exchange of numbers, nothing. I went home confused but fifty dollars richer come Monday.

The next day, my dad kept asking if I had a good time and if I did, why I wasn't calling her for another date. I waited until about seven and found her number, so I called her. She was doing laundry and cleaning, so I kept the conversation short. Again, no real excitement or discussion of another date. My dad was so upset with me. He thought for sure I should have another date that night. Finally, my mom came to my rescue. He always had a corny pickup line he wanted me to use. He would tell me to say, "Hi, I thought I would see if you wanted to get a coke or something." The first time I heard that, I thought to myself, *This isn't 1960.* There has got to be something better than that out there. However, after thinking about Beth for more than an hour, I decided to call her back. This time, I pulled out the corny pickup line. "Hey, I was thinking about getting out tomorrow and riding around, so I thought I would see if you wanted to get out and maybe get a coke or something." When I shut up, I was sweating buckets plus I was waiting for the comeback of "not interested." In her very tired voice, she said, "I don't know. I will have to see what time I get up and how I feel, but call me tomorrow about eleven."

Okay, it wasn't no, but it wasn't yes, so I guess his line didn't get me hung up on. Sunday morning, I called her as she asked, and this time, she seemed a little more alert. After I asked her if she was interested, she said yep, and so we had our second date, and Monday wasn't here yet, so did this mean I would get a hundred bucks? We went out to lunch, rode around and looked at houses, ate dinner, and went to a late movie, which she slept through. I thought, *Well, if she sleeps on my shoulder, then maybe she is interested, but if she doesn't, then I am out come tomorrow.* It was another long day and night. I took her home after the movie and said good night. Again, no kiss, no hand holding, nothing.

Monday morning, we both went to school and didn't really talk that much, so I thought for sure the end was upon us. During the break, we talked a little, and again, it seemed like there might be some interest. I found the guy with the bet and told him. He couldn't believe it, so he had to ask Beth. I was hoping she would give me a kiss on the cheek in front of him just to add insult to injury, but she, very nonchalantly, acknowledged we went out. To this day, I never have received any money, and I never expected it. This guy was really into Beth, so my winning is December 2, 1994—I made her my wife.

We were married for about nine months, then we started talking about having kids, starting a family. Our thought process for starting young was so we could still enjoy them when they were in their early twenties even if this meant we might struggle at first. I remember going to my in-laws to tell them the news. They were so excited to become grandparents nine months later.

On May 31, 1996, at around 8:00 p.m., Beth started feeling like it was time to deliver the baby. I took her to Baptist Memorial Hospital East in Memphis, Tennessee. She laid there for many hours with discomfort. She was having a planned C-section, so we didn't know how long they would allow her to be in labor before going ahead with the procedure. At about midnight—now it's June

1—the doctor on call told us he is discharging her because there hasn't been any change in her cervix. I politely told him, "We would not be going home? She is having a C-section. She is in pain. We are here. Why not do it now?" At about 3:30, June 1, 1996, Beth and I welcomed Thomas Brady Jones into the world via C-section. He was healthy, and she was resting well.

Brady grew at a normal pace. He walked on time and started talking just as he should. We were spoiled and lucky. He was such an easy and happy baby. He slept through the night from about six weeks on. We could put him in bed about seven thirty or eight, and he would sleep until about six the next morning.

When Brady was almost two, we had an opportunity to relocate to Denver, Colorado. I don't think this was a fan-favorite decision for some, but I had an opportunity to grow in my career with more chances of advancement, so I took it. We put our house up for sale and moved. We ended up living with my brother Troy, his wife, and two daughters in a three-bedroom apartment. It was tight, and it was a lot of togetherness, but we did it. After our house sold, we moved into a three-story townhouse in Greenwood Village. It was a great place.

After twelve months there, we moved into a rental in Highland Ranch. Brady now had a large yard to play in, plus Beth was now pregnant with our second child. We—really Beth—was so excited to be having a baby girl. We had the nursery decorated in pink from floor to ceiling. Beth had five ultrasounds, so we were pretty certain we would have a little girl. On January 20, 2000, Beth gave birth via another C-section to William Thomas Jones—funny girl name. When the doctor pulled the baby out, there was no girl; it was a boy. God knew I couldn't handle a girl, or maybe he knew we would need a strong boy in a few years.

Brady was so excited to be the big brother. We still sit down with the kids today and reminisce about that day. I had to leave the hospital, rush home, and repaint the nursery. I also had to return the girl clothes for boy clothes, including getting a "go home" outfit. My mother in-law, Mary, was there, so that was a big help. A few days later, Beth and Will came home. Now, we were a family of four.

Will grew like Brady, on time with everything—walking, talking, running, etc. Brady was a great big brother. He liked feeding him, holding him, and trying to get him to play. Brady would show him his toys, but of course, Will was just a little guy. However, there would be a severe role reversal between these two brothers.

It all began eight years ago in Denver, Colorado, during 2005. Brady had just turned nine, and Will was five and a half years old. Both the boys liked to ride their bikes; of course, Will had to use training wheels. They loved playing outside with their friends. We had kids on both sides of us who also went to the same school and were close in age. Brady had just learned how to ride a dirt bike that a friend of ours let us use. One day, after several attempts, Brady was riding with no fear. I was a hobby motocross rider and knew it was dangerous, but to see my son riding and doing something he had wanted to do for so long was just amazing, especially since it only took him about one hour to get it. Five days later, we weren't focusing on riding motorcycles anymore.

No, No, No

In Highlands Ranch, Colorado, school is on a "track" system. School is all year-round through middle school. "Yuck," Brady would say. It was not that bad. The kids would go for three to five weeks on, then off for two to three weeks, on for six to nine weeks, off for five weeks, and so forth.

The day was Friday, June 10, 2005, five days before the school year ended and Brady would be a third grader. I was working for an architectural firm down on Sherman Street near Seventh Avenue. Beth was a stay-at-home mom and was going to the school to eat with Brady. The weather was cloudy with a chance for heavy rain. The firm I was working for changed the working hours from Memorial Day to Labor Day, so on Friday's, I had the opportunity to leave around noon if my workload and clients allowed.

I had just left the office and was heading down Broadway. I turned on I-25 heading south for our home in Highlands Ranch. As I approached the I-225 and I-25 interchange, I received a phone call from Beth. She was scared to death. She said, "I just got a call from the school, and Brady was not responding, so they had to call 911. They need us to meet them at Sky Ridge Medical Center in Lone Tree. I just left the school like twenty minutes ago. I just ate with him." Just as I heard those words, the bottom fell out of the sky. The rain was so hard, I could barely see. Here I am, a scared father, trying to figure out what happened, driving approximately eighty miles an hour with my hazards on in the pouring rain. I kept saying to myself, "I have to get to the hospital and get control of the situation to make sure Brady is in the best care possible. I have to be strong for Beth, Will, and Brady."

Will is our youngest son. At the time of the stroke, he was only five. He didn't understand why he couldn't see his brother or why he had to go spend the night with our friends, the Stantons, who lived next door to us. Cheryl was great with Will, and she had several kids of her own, so we knew he would be in good hands.

I was the first to arrive at the hospital. I approached the desk, and they sent me back. What I saw next brought me to my knees. When I turned the corner, I was expecting to see my son lying there, crying because he was scared and have some kind of bone injury. I would comfort him, and when Beth got there, everything would be fine. Quite the opposite happened.

When I entered the ER where Brady was at 1:30 p.m., he was not talking, moving, or crying—nothing. I thought he was going to die. He would wake up for a short bit, look at me, and then fade back out again. This must have continued for what seemed like hours but was probably only about one to two hours in total.

After I took a few minutes with him, the doctors and staff began asking me questions about his health history and family history. Beth showed up within minutes, and she and I just sat and cried with one another because we did not know what had happened. What would be next? Is he going to make it, or has GOD prepared a place for him? Later, we realized God was not ready for our son yet, and he had a plan and had given us a story to share with others.

After some time passed, we finally had a chance to speak with the paramedics who brought him in to the ER. They were very concerned for our son when they arrived at the school. They knew this was not a seizure they were dealing with and it was more serious than expected. They had a small child in a coma state—not having seizures. They told us the 911 call came in from his school, Arrowwood Elementary. The caller told the 911 operator there was a young boy that was having what appeared to be seizures and was not responding. The dispatcher sent the paramedics immediately. When they arrived, they were shocked at the original 911 call and the information given. Most of us are not doctors and shouldn't play one during the day. This was a life-or-death situation that got played off as some minor seizure.

After Beth and I heard this news from the paramedics, we wanted to speak with the school. Within minutes of us talking with the doctors and paramedics, we had our chance to visit the principal of the school. She had come to the ER to ensure us the school was on top of everything and the situation was handled properly. That was the last thing I was worried about at this point. Glad to see the school was only concerned about letting us know they handled the situation properly. Thanks for the update!

After being at the ER for several hours, the PE teacher came to the hospital where we got her story. Brady had just entered the gym for PE. When the kids entered the gym, they are usually still in a line from walking in the halls. They were only second graders. After entering the gym, Brady turned to his best friend, Alex, and said, "My brain hurts!" That was it. Brady fell to the gym floor, hitting his face and head on the floor and scratching his face with his glasses. "My brain hurts" is a phrase I hope I never hear again. The PE teacher tried to get Brady to wake up, but he would not. After a minute or so, she picked Brady up where he finally came to and was grabbing at her from one side. She carried him to the nurse's station where they called 911.

I see a problem with this method of care from the school. Why wasn't the PE teacher the one at the hospital first? Why was the PE teacher sent back to class when she was the one who was trying to care for him? We began to ask all valid questions while we were in the ER.

The bigger problem was the ER staff could not find what was wrong with Brady. They continued to monitor Brady and wait for him to wake up again. They would say, "Well, seizures are very common in children, and he will wake up in a few minutes."

"What are a few minutes to you?" I asked. Brady only regained consciousness one time, but when he did, he could not talk. Nothing. The nurse would not take the neck brace off until he told her his neck did not hurt. Another problem—we all realized he could not talk. All he could do was cry. He was scared. He had two IVs in

his arm; he could not move his other arm, foot, leg—
nothing. Absolutely nothing!

Our time in the ER was less than stellar. The ER
doctor found it necessary to leave when her shift was
over and leave Brady with someone who had not been
around him rather than to stay and work to find out what
was wrong. Beth and I were asking for an MRI because
we knew this test would give a more detailed look into
him. We were told, "An MRI is not typically used in an
emergency situation, especially when we have a patient
that is not stable. We did a CAT scan, and that is 90
percent accurate and shows everything we need. A CT
scan of the brain may also be used to evaluate the effects
of treatment on brain tumors and to detect clots in the
brain that may be responsible for strokes."

Finally, at about 3:30 p.m., we were told the new
ER doctor was transferring Brady to another hospital
since Sky Ridge was not equipped to handle Brady's
case. "Okay. So what is wrong with him?" we asked. The
doctor told us he did not know but that Sky Ridge was
not the place for him. At about 5:30 p.m., we received
Brady's transfer papers, and the ambulance was about to
load him up and take him to Swedish Medical Center
in Englewood. Why Swedish and not Children's, I am
not sure, but at least we would find out the answer to
"What happened?"

It's a Stroke, What?

J ust before 6 p.m. on Friday, June 10, we all arrived at
Swedish Medical Center. Beth was with Brady in the
ambulance, so she got to enter with him. I had to enter
through the ER where there was a security guard trying
to point me in the direction of my son. As I was still in
shock, I found myself wondering the halls, attempting to
find where they took my wife and son, and after about
fifteen minutes, I was finally reunited with them.

They were met by a pediatric intensivist named Dr.
Bernard. It did not take long for him to examine Brady
to tell something was really wrong. He told us he was
calling in a neurologist by the name of Dr. Miller. Dr.
Bernard spoke to us about a few things it could be. He
mentioned Brady could be having a severe migraine; he
could just have been hit in the head, but it appears he has
had a stroke.

He was going to send Brady down for an MRI—
imagine that—and wait for Dr. Miller to arrive. Brady
was in the MRI for about forty-five minutes, and we
waited in the waiting area until he was through. While

we were waiting, Tim Johnson, Brady's teacher arrived. He sat with us and asked us what we knew at that point. He was close with Brady, so this was not easy for him either. We told him that Brady possibly had a stroke, then Tim's jaw dropped to the floor. Tim was in as much shock as we were. "A nine-year-old can suffer a stroke like this?" Tim asked. "I guess so," Beth answered.

While Beth and I watched our young boy lay in an MRI tube, all we could do was weep as we were scared for him and what all this would mean. Beth just kept saying, "This is like one horrible dream." You are not kidding. The MRI seemed to take forever. Finally, we were reunited with Brady, but he still couldn't talk, so all we could do is talk to him and rub our hands on his head. He knew something was really wrong with him. Tim also was with us when Brady came out, and Brady just smiled ear to ear. He was real close to ol' Mr. Tim Johnson. As time would show, they would get a lot closer.

Once Dr. Miller reviewed the MRI/MRA (magnetic resonance imaging/magnetic resonance angiogram), there was only one thing that could cause this much damage to Brady's brain and bring us to our knees. Dr. Miller informed us Brady had indeed suffered a massive stroke, and unfortunately, since he was having the stroke for so long, it was way too late to do anything for him other than plan for a long recovery. Brady had complete loss of speech, use of his right arm and leg, and he had a large area of brain damage from the lack of oxygen to the brain for so long. In addition, Brady had some brain swelling, which needed to be monitored very closely. At this point, we had the diagnosis and needed to start informing others. We asked Dr. Miller to explain to us what the next few days, weeks, or months would look like for Brady. For the next seventy-two hours, Brady was going to be in ICU, so he could get a blood thinner in his body. We spent Friday evening through Monday morning in the ICU with Brady. An ICU is typically not known for allowing too many people in the patient's room, but the hospital made an exception since he was so young. During our stay in ICU, Brady had several other doctors review his case, his heart, and his blood. They were searching for what could have caused this to happen and at a young age.

On Saturday, while the doctors did their thing, we would ask questions and try to learn as much as we could about Brady's situation and what to expect. Mr. Johnson came back that morning and brought a little red sponge ball. He had Brady throwing with his left hand in a matter of minutes. I am not sure ICU was the place to be teaching him how to throw left-handed, but we didn't care as long as Brady was comfortable. The night before, Beth and I called our parents to explain what happened with Brady. Of course, like all grandparents and parents, they were on the first flight Saturday morning to comfort us and be with Brady. Beth's parents, Larry and Mary Phillips of Memphis, were able to get to the hospital first thing Saturday. My first sight of them was my father-in-law holding his little girl in his arms as she cried with my mother-in-law holding on to her. I don't care what we may go through in life; being able to cuddle in your parents' arms for comfort can be a real help.

All parents should remember that because, sometimes, words don't even have to be said to be comforted. A simple hug or smile can be just as effective. It wasn't long after when my parents, David and Barbara Jones, who lived in Mississippi at the time, arrived at the hospital. A good friend or ours, Andy Krenek, was willing to pick them up from the airport and bring them to the hospital. This wasn't a short drive. The airport is clear out near West Kansas, and the hospital is located off Hampden toward the Front Range. Andy is a great person with a great family. We had known each other for several years. His wife Kirie and I worked together in 1998 when we moved to Denver. Although, they have one major flaw; they are Bears fans. Anytime the Bears played, I always rooted for the other team just to get Andy stirred up.

As everyone arrived and several calls from friends came in, no one could understand what actually happened to Brady the day before. Strokes in kids are very rare to the point doctors don't even understand them and the possible treatments. We were all left wondering what would be next for Brady.

Our First Stay

With ICU being pretty strict on visitors, Beth and I made sure we were by Brady's side as much as possible. We would take a walk to the cafeteria or to the waiting room to talk on the phone, or we would just walk. Our parents were there with us, so they helped us keep calm. Larry, my father-in-law, had just started a new job in Memphis, so he was only able to stay until Monday. Mary, my mother-in-law, and my parents were prepared to stay for the week, and even longer if needed.

They would take turns going home to rest and taking care of our two bassett hounds. Max was just a puppy, so he needed a lot of care. By this point, all of our neighbors had been notified, so they were all wanting to help with yard work, dogs, and anything else we needed. We lived on a street with some of the best friends and neighbors in America. The Lance, Alldredge, and Stanton family will always hold a special piece of my heart.

During Brady's stay in ICU, the hospital, Swedish Medical Center, had to call in nurses for Brady. See, there were no kids in this hospital at the time, as far as the pediatric floor was concerned. There were plenty of adults in ICU. There was an elderly woman who we just thought was waiting for our Lord to take her home, but the interesting part was the next day, she was sitting up in her chair and talking like nothing was wrong. She was a nice lady, but her recovery was very strange.

On June 13, Brady completed his seventy-two hours of heparin in the ICU; he was then transferred up to the pediatric floor. Brady had his own nursing staff for several days. Even though he still could not talk, he liked being the only patient and having a great medical staff caring for him. Over the next few days, Beth and I would spend a lot of time with Dr. Miller and others trying to determine the recovery protocol for Brady. Swedish Medical Center was not the place for Brady to recover because he needed lots of physical, occupational, and speech therapy. It was clear we needed to transfer Brady to Children's Hospital of Denver. One problem— Children's Hospital did not have any room for Brady. So we all spent several days on the fourth floor at Swedish Medical Center until Children's Hospital was ready.

Brady didn't do any real therapy while at Swedish Medical since we were trying to get him a spot at Children's; however, the nurses and doctors had a few exercises and tests they gave him while he was there. It wasn't until about three days after his stroke when he murmured his first word. All parents get competitive over who the baby will call out to first—mommy or daddy. At this point, there was no competitive nature between Beth and me as we were just so happy when he said the word *phone*. "Phone?" I asked. He just laid there and pointed toward a glass or his mom. We became very good at reading our son's mind.

After many hours and days of speech therapy, *phone* would be the main word for everything until Brady got much better,. It was very tiring for all of us, even the nurses struggled some. Tomorrow, when you get up, try going two hours using only one word to communicate. Impossible.

At this point, I had been off work for almost a week, and to be honest, I wasn't even thinking about work. All Beth and I could focus on was getting our son better. A few of my teammates from the office came by a few times while we were at Swedish Medical Center. Sean even brought his famous breakfast burritos. We had those every day and night for several days. He must have made two or three dozen. Tim Johnson came by and played catch with Brady and tried to get our mind off things. He was truly a blessing from above, for Brady and us, during Brady's recovery.

On June 15, Brady finally transferred to Children's Hospital of Denver, and we still had no clue as to why he had a stroke. Here we were, five days after the stroke and no medical reason for our nine-year-old to suffer a stroke other than a clot formed in his little brain. Most people would say that is the cause. Well, they might be right, but there was no reason for the clot to form. Brady wasn't hit in the head, had not fallen, and there was no trace of a clot moving through his body or heart. All those tests came up negative. It was finally time for Brady to transfer to his third hospital in seven days.

Start of Recovery

As I continue to write our story, I find myself at my desk, reliving Brady's tough road ahead, and I can visualize everything about those five weeks like they just happened, not to mention my late grandmother saved every care page post I had written to update people with Brady's progress.

When Brady arrived at Children's Hospital, there still wasn't room for him, but we were able to get a semiprivate room for the first day to get him started seeing the rehab doctors and learning about the hospital stay.

On that Friday, one week after his stroke, Brady was moved to a private room with some of the best nurses in the medical field. At the age of nine, most of us liked everyone, but when it came to doctors, we ran the other way. Brady was no different, but the staff at Children's was so good to build a relationship with Brady, so he knew he could trust them and they wouldn't harm him; they were there to help him get better.

The first week at Children's was a real learning experience for us. At the time, my father-in-law had already returned to Tennessee, so my parents and mother-in-law had the pleasure of being around for support. I remember sitting at the foot of the bed the first afternoon at Children's and breaking down to tears in front of them all; I am not usually one to do this, but when your son is lying there, hardly able to communicate, it hits, and it hits hard. My dad is not a very emotional person, but on this day, he did the one thing he had not done in many years, and that was comfort me in a time of darkness. I was asking God why he let this happen. I was screaming with anger. When my father put his hand on my shoulder, it was like God was speaking to me through him. His touch, his voice, and his words were so comforting. This was very strange for me since I had never heard God speak to me more than he did that day.

> In him we were also chosen, having been predestined according to the plan of him who works out everything in conformity with the purpose of his will, in order that we, who were the first to put our hope in Christ, might be for the praise of his glory.
>
> Ephesians 1:11–12 (TNIV)

What has happened to Brady is God's plan for him, and the more I fight against it or try to go left when he needs me to go right, the more troubled I feel. I have an empty feeling. I am not at peace inside. After I internalized the teachings of his word, I found myself more at peace and ready to push forward for Brady, Will, and Beth. They needed me as much as I needed them.

After getting settled in with the staff and surroundings, the fun really began. For Beth, she got the opportunity to visit with a very *nice* lady from the insurance department. The lady was asking about additional insurance we may need or something. Beth wasn't even thinking about this, and the lady said something else, which made Beth just about loose her cool. It's a good thing Beth walked away from the conflict because I am not sure what would have happened. Over an hour had passed, so I went looking for her, only to find her sitting in another patient's room, talking with the other patient's parents. She was so steamed over what the insurance lady did or said; another parent witnessed it and asked her to sit with her for a while. Not only were the doctors and nurses so friendly, but even the parents of other patients were outstanding. We were all there trying to cope with what our child was going through.

On Saturday of that week, Brady began his rehab program. He had rehab therapy six hours a day, six days a week. We lived in the hospital for four weeks. Once we got all the schedules and some idea of what we were up against, my parents left to return to Mississippi. My mother-in-law was able to stay for several weeks to help with Will and give us some breaks at the hospital. She ended up leaving around June 24 and taking Will with her to Tennessee. Will stayed with Larry and Mary for three weeks before Mary flew back to Denver with him. At his age, this was a very difficult thing to do, but Brady needed me and Beth. Both of our kids love spending time with both sets of grandparents, so it worked out, but I can't imagine what Will must have thought being gone from his mommy for that long.

Brady's typical day for rehab

7:30 a.m. – breakfast group with occupational therapists
8:00 a.m. – speech therapy
10:00 a.m. – physical therapy
11:00 a.m. – break for lunch and nap
1:30 p.m. – speech therapy
2:30 p.m. – occupational therapy
4:00 p.m. – physical therapy

At approximately five or five thirty each day, he would finish from his long day of rehab. After the first full week at Children's Hospital, he was still confined to a wheel chair, barely speaking, and not able to use his right arm or hand, although the therapists were doing everything they could to try to move the right arm and leg. The cool thing about all of this was we learned our son has got a lot of fight in him. He was unwavering in his passion to walk out of that hospital when he left.

> Today, June 20, 2005, Brady has some minor movement in his right hip and leg. The leg will continue to be worked on as well as the right arm. Brady is in therapy 6 times a day to try and get his functions back again. He starts his day at 7:30 and ends around 5:00 with a small break around lunch. Brady's spirits continue to be up and down as does ours. We are so thankful to Larry and Mary Phillips, David and Barbara Jones, the Kephart family and many others for

their continued support and gracious time each
has offered. We look forward to a full recovery
that doctors say may take up to a full year.

—Posted by Tommy Jones on
Brady Jones's care page

The last sentence hits really hard. At first, the doctors
were telling us of a full recovery but that Brady would
need to work hard and focus on getting better. As we all
know, things change.

Middle of the Road

Room 520 was located right across from the nurses' station. Right behind the nurses' station was a small library with a desktop computer for those looking for internet connection for e-mails or posting care page updates. Like most hospitals, this floor had the nurses' station located in the middle, with the patient rooms on the outside walls in a square, so you could say Brady was located about the middle of the road. The public bathrooms, though, were located around the nurses' station—on the left, down the hall, take another left, then walk about thirty paces. Even though Brady had a shared bathroom for him and his neighbor patient, the parents and visitors were really not supposed to use it, so Beth and I made routine hikes to use the facilities. Occasionally, during the night, we would use the in-room bathroom, but it wasn't very often. There was nothing like waking from a dead sleep, grabbing your slippers, and making the dreaded walk to the bathroom in the middle of the night with your nighttime bed head. This was a very common occurrence, so the nurses on duty never really paid any attention to any of the parents.

The hours turned into days, which turned into weeks. After the first week, we had a better understanding of the routine, but we were still left wondering what happened and asking why this happened. I remember the first Tuesday at Children's because this was the day Brady began to get a little of his old personality back. He was getting more and more frustrated with being in the hospital. At this point, he was doing very well with rehab. The one drawback was Brady had to get two shots a day of Lovenox to treat his blood. He not only had a neurologist and therapist, he also had a hematologist to study his blood make-up to see if there were any reasons for the stroke. This doctor wanted Brady to take the shots to keep his blood from clotting in the future until more test could be completed.

Mary came to the hospital and gave Beth and me a much-needed break. We were able to get something to eat, sit alone, and visit about everything that had happened over the past ten to twelve days. At this point, it still felt like a horrible dream. "How could a kid full of life suddenly become a kid who is stuck in a shell of who he used to be?" I would ask. Beth and I had several meetings with all of his doctors in the same room. This helped us get a better understanding from the whole team at once. There were times when one doctor would say something and another doctor would contradict what he/she said. So I had to stop the meeting and call everyone out on it and find out who was right and what we should believe. For those of us who have been in this type of situation before, getting confusing information is a big no-no. Let's make sure everyone is in agreement before we bring a patient or their family into the conversation. As a caregiver, we are already confused enough.

At our first doctors' meeting, we were hit in the face with the truth about our son's recovery. The doctors informed us Brady would be at Children's at least four to six more weeks. Most rehab patients were going home in two to three weeks, so we knew this was not a typical protocol and the doctors were perplexed about the situation. We also learned the doctors were especially concerned about his speech and his arm. What was originally deemed a full recovery and could take up to a year was now being reduced to "Brady may never get any better." As the meeting continued, we were able to understand the recovery will come, but his arm may never come back because the brain has essentially been disconnected from the arm. In addition, the speech therapist was really concerned about his learning and several of his speech tests; however, his leg was improving. The therapist got Brady a walker so he could start trying to walk on his own versus the wheelchair. Brady was due to be back to school on August 12 and had a long way to go if that would become reality.

At this point in Brady's hospital stay, we were asking for friends and family to come by as often as they could to see Brady so he could have some normalcy to his days. Mr. Johnson came by all the time. He even spent the night with Brady so Beth and I could go home and use our own shower and sleep in a normal bed. Our sleeping arrangements in room 520 were not five-star hotel-like. There was a window seat that Beth and I would sleep on in a spoon position, considering that was the only way we fit. I am six three and almost 220 pounds. The window seat was about five feet six inches long and not wide enough for even me. There was also a recliner in Brady's room sometimes so one of us would get in it for a while. Although Brady was the one going through the hard work and actual pain when getting shots or giving blood, he seemed to have no problem sleeping. I believe he slept some of his best sleep while in the hospital.

On June 26, some sixteen days after his stroke, we received our first good news. Brady's blood work all came back negative or normal from all of the tests. This was a huge milestone because we knew there was nothing medically wrong with him, which we had been very concerned about. A friend of Brady's came by and spent several hours with him. Brady even took them on a walk around the floor. He struggled a bit with using the walker, and he got extremely tired, but he did well. At one point, I had to catch him because he wanted to walk faster than the leg would actually move. Also, by this time, the doctors had determined that he could be off the shots and get on some oral type of medicine to continue regulating his blood; however, the doctor ended up putting a port in his leg for the shots instead of changing his medicine. The port is neat in a way. It allows the nurse to administer the injections without actually getting stuck with a needle. If my dad had to do this, he would have already gone on to heaven. He is so afraid of needles. He will die being afraid of needles. As I am writing, I am waiting for him to get a doctor's appointment because he has some bleeding behind one of his eyes. He found out when he called to make the appointment that the doctor may want to inject him with some dye or something, so he didn't make the appointment. We all have things we don't like or are scared of, but when it comes to life or death, I believe I would be taking the advice of my doctors, pops.

> "You believe at last!" Jesus answered. "But a time is coming, and has come, when you will be scattered, each to his own home. You will leave me all alone. Yet I am not alone, for my Father is with me." "I have told you these things, so that in me you may have peace. In this world you will have trouble. But take heart! I have overcome the world."
>
> John 16:31–33 (NIV)

When I read this some many years after Brady's stroke, I call back to the early stages of his recovery and am reminded by the scripture that we will face trouble. We will need to overcome adversity, sadness, and sorrow, but he overcame the world and many who sought him for his crucifixion. I also have learned through my journey with Christ, there is great peace in him. We can't find peace in material things, money, lust, or other sinful paths. The only peace is to surrender all to Christ and lean on him in our darkest, trying times. God is always working and will show his plan at the right time. I needed to be reminded I was not alone in this journey. and neither was Brady. We both had a God watching over us and guiding the doctors and Brady to a path that would be his new life as a child and later as an adult.

At about halfway in Brady's recovery, we were growing more and more optimistic about Brady's outcome and future. June 29, we got to see Brady move his arm for the first time, which brought joy and tears to my face. Also, this day, the speech therapist showed us how Brady could speak more and take on more sentence structure. He was becoming more accurate with cue cards and visual cues. Not only was he getting stronger and improving in rehab, we were finally hearing some proposed release dates for Brady.

July 20 was the target, which was almost another month, but at least we had something to hope for and Brady could see the light at the end of the tunnel. It is so hard to be successful if you don't have an expectation, target date, or a metric in which to measure your success. Being in the architectural industry, this is a prerequisite in order to be good at our job; you have to be able to communicate these things to clients and employees. It is the same thing with most other things in life. We all can put our head down to achieve great things as long as we know and understand what the overall plan or outcome will be. I believe most of us work even harder when we know the plan or can predict the outcome. However, attempting to predict the future is pretty difficult. I have tried to do this to please employers for years, and I am batting about .250 on success. Employers and clients might wake up one day and decide the work you just did isn't what they want anymore, so now you may be headed in another direction to please them. "Where the heck did this come from?" I would ask.

Simple Things

A dult time. What does this mean to you? I know, for me, it could mean so many things—a simple dinner with my beautiful wife, lunch with a friend, play eighteen holes of golf, whatever I wanted to do for myself and with other adults. Is it bad to want some time away from our children? Is it bad to need a break from three weeks in the hospital? Even though I was torn on this, I had others tell me that in order to stay strong for Brady and the rest of the family, Beth and I would need to find some time out of the hospital, out of the rehab schedule, and away from the whole situation. A break is a good thing and should never be looked at as a sign of weakness. It has taken me eight years to realize this, and it has been a tough lesson. I have always been the one who thought people who needed a break from something must we weak, must not have the strength to deal with their situation, or was just plain silly. Oh, how wrong I was.

July 2 was a fun day for me. Two guys from the office, Paul and Doug, came by to catch up and check on Brady. They really showed their support for my family. Doug usually doesn't show emotion, but as a father of two close to my kid's age, this might have stirred him up. They had come by to insure me they were thinking about us and to take as much time as I needed to get back. For all of us in the working world, this is huge, considering I only wanted to focus on Brady and his recovery and not work. I am sure I could have gone to the office one to two days a week, but they didn't push me.

The day before, Mike and Jaye brought up a very nice dinner, and even a bottle of wine, which we all shared. It was nice. One of Brady's nurses watched him while we went to the courtyard with Mike and Jaye to enjoy some adult conversation and great food. Jaye is pretty funny, and Mike is very laid back. Jaye even came to the hospital to read to Brady several times and allowed us a break. They lived very close to the office and hospital, so they gave us a key to their place and told us we could come by any time to grab a shower. People don't realize that it is these little things that they do that mean the world. I would have never asked them, but they offered, so it was so good to have a place to get away to rather than driving twenty-five miles back to our house. One day, we took them up on their offer and went to shower at their house. Mike, being an architect, had done a great job with remodeling their house over the years. The bathroom was no exception. The shower was approximately four by six with a center rain head and shower head on the wall. There was a very large seat in the shower. We had just enough time to catch showers and get back to the hospital before Brady finished his morning rehab appointments. It was all the little things that really made a difference in my outlook each day. To this day, I am not sure they realize how special it was for them to offer the use of their place.

Brady was granted a pass to leave the hospital for July 4 since there was no therapy that day. The doctors and therapist team really thought it would be good to get him out of the hospital and in the public to see how he responds, but we had to be careful not to get him in situations with too much stimuli. We invited the Stantons from next door. Alex was Brady's best friend, and he was with Brady the moment Brady suffered his stroke. Since we all parted ways in December 2006, I never have understood how Alex dealt with Brady's stroke. Being with someone one minute and them being in an ambulance the next has got to be very scary, especially for a young child.

We all went to lunch at one of Brady's favorite restaurants—Hops. I don't believe the chain is still around. It was a good place to eat. It was similar to J. Alexander's. After lunch, we took Brady to Cherry Creek Mall to ride around in the wheelchair the hospital had loaned us for the day. The riding lasted about ten minutes, then he wanted to walk. This was concerning to me because if Brady took a fall, he could injure himself and possibly have a bleed in the brain, and being on the Lovenox, this was very dangerous. A tear-jerking moment for me was when I asked Brady to try and hold my hand, and he did with his right hand. He was even able to squeeze a little. This was a huge sign from God that he was working to heal Brady but was also a reminder that he still had a long way to go. While we were at the mall, we bought Brady some new shoes for his therapy and walking in the hospital. He just smiled when he got them. Brady still is and has always been a shoe person. He loves all kinds of shoes. Mr. Stanton bought Brady a PSP handheld game device to see if that would inspire him to try to use the hand. The gesture was very nice, and Brady tried like hell to play the thing. I don't believe he ever really gave up trying as much as it was a reminder he had something wrong with him.

The day really wore him out. He did a bit of walking, trying to talk, and there was a lot of stimuli at the mall, so his brain was on overload. We took him back to the hospital and tried to see the fireworks from Coors Field. The parking garage of the hospital wasn't far, and the nurses would take the kids up there for the annual fireworks show. The Colorado Rockies put on a great show. They would send the fireworks over the back of the centerfield wall, and it could be seen for miles. Since Children's Hospital was located at the opposite end of downtown, we had a very good view. However, the game went late, and Brady had enough for one day, so we called it a night and went to bed with him. This was really the first long day for him, and his endurance was not there to take on more time-out. He didn't have a nap that day, so we knew it was time to go in.

It seemed like Christmas in July. Brady got shoes and video games, but he also got a very large care package from Pro Circuit in California. Pro Circuit is an engine, suspension, and motocross modification company located in Corona, California. I had the chance to meet Travis from Pro Circuit when I organized a fund-raiser for pediatric cancer only five days before Brady's stroke. Travis had put together a box with a Team Pro Circuit jersey, videos, stickers, and even a backpack, which we still use today for different things. This box probably wouldn't be much for some people, but to Brady, it was a lot for someone who cared enough to send him something to cheer him up. He smiled for days and watched all the videos when he wasn't in therapy. Pro Circuit wasn't the only people to send him something. A representative for the energy drink Go Fast brought two cases of their drink for us to keep going. We drank some of it, but it was the gesture and the thought that was heartfelt. These people were sponsors of the fund-raiser I put on, so this was a step above doing something for us and Brady like this.

As kids and adults, we all like getting material gifts like the items I mentioned, but I have to admit, the intangible items, for me, were the endless hours people gave of their time to come visit us, help take our minds off the situation, allow Beth and me to take a break, and the e-mails and phone calls we received. As I have mentioned before, strokes in children are very rare, so not too many people knew what the recovery would be like, or even that it was a big deal. Brady's stroke is so different than most strokes in children. Because of this, people from all around the world were sending e-mails and posting messages on his care page. That is what mattered to me and one of the things that helped me get up when I was down. Even today, we have people who still show compassion for the situation we have been dealing with for the last eight years. Oddly enough, there are also some people who ask what happened, and when you tell them, they just say, "Oh," like it was nothing and everything is normal. Oh, I wish that was the case.

Home Stretch

July 7, 2005—Brady was in the home stretch. Most would think this a great feeling, but Brady was getting very nervous because this meant no more nurses to care for him around-the-clock. He was going to be stuck with Mom and Dad. He had become very close to, two of his nurses. Stephanie was mostly a daytime nurse, but did work some nights, but there was the male nurse who typically took the nighttime shifts. I wish I could remember his name. At some point, Brady really built a connection with him, and Beth and I could go home to sleep in our own bed a few times a week. The catch was we had to be back before he woke up and went to rehab. One morning, we were running late to the hospital, and Brady had already gotten up, went to the bathroom, and got dressed with the nurse. By the time we got there, he was already in therapy. Brady got a little worried about where we were and if we would return. Going through something like this can test a family and a person's faith in God, but hopefully, the dedication they have for one another is enough to make it. We heard horror stories where the parents of small children facing an illness would just walk away and never come back. It might be the mom, the dad, or in severe cases, both. The child is suffering the illness, left to fight it alone, and the parents decide they can't handle it and don't come back. What could be more horrifying than that for a child?

Once we arrived at the hospital, we went straight to see him in therapy. I saw a scared boy sitting there, working hard, but the look on his face told me everything I needed to know. My family is my rock, and I will always do everything in my power to protect them and to care for them. I vowed to myself I would do whatever I could to help spread the word about pediatric stroke. There needs to be more awareness about the issue so others might be able to have a better outcome than Brady did on June 10.

Brady was granted another leave for the day from hospital. This time it was with his therapist and a trip to the zoo. Brady showed he wanted to walk and was determined to no matter what it looked like. He knew it wasn't normal, but he was walking anyway. He rode in the wheelchair for only a few feet, then he popped up and walked. His determination to do things played a big part in his recovery up to this point and even beyond. Around this time, he started opening and shutting his hand, raising his arm, and speaking more. This was almost four weeks since his stroke.

Brady was fitted for his orthotic foot brace. The purpose of the brace was to keep his foot engaged and not have it droop so much. The foot drop caused him to trip more often, so having the device on this lower leg helped him walk, maintain a better balance, and kept him a bit safer. Brady's safety after he left the hospital was most important for everyone involved. Another concern before getting released was his INR (international normalized ratio) levels. We didn't want to leave the hospital with having to give Brady shots twice a day if we didn't have to. I knew I would be the one doing it because Beth gets very faint in situations like that. During the last few days prior to being discharged, I had to start practicing by giving him the shot through his port. The port would not be going home with us, so I was going to have to give Brady his shot in the arm if required. I have a newfound respect for those who have to do this on a regular basis for whatever reason.

Eventually, we were able to get Brady moved off the shots and taking an oral medicine, Coumadin. The problem with this medicine was the instability of keeping his blood regulated, so Brady would have blood draws frequently. We were ready for whatever he needed to continue his recovery and help him get better, including dragging him to give blood. The next few weeks would tell us what would happen upon his discharge. We already knew he would be facing close to a year of continued rchab, so throwing on a few more appointments wasn't a big deal in his situation.

An acquaintance told me to accept help from those who offered. I have a lot of pride to the point it can be viewed as stubborn. However, some people had wanted to give money to help with Brady's continued outpatient rehab. I finally agreed to accept it, and we were able to raise some money to help, and it was greatly appreciated. My view on this, after living through it, is this: accept any help whether it's financially, spiritually, meals, or anything in between. Pride can get in the way and sometimes can create blindness. I never thought we needed the money, but that is how some people wanted to show their support.

We found out Brady would be released on July 15, 2005, about three to four days earlier than expected. This was a great day for me as it was also my thirty-third birthday. This was going to be the best present I could ask for—taking my boy home. I was holding out hope he would go home even sooner, but it was not up to me; it was up to God. We learn through his Word to trust in God's timing.

> There is a time for everything, and a season for every activity under heaven.
>
> Ecclesiastes 3:1 (NIV)

> He has made everything beautiful in its time. He has also set eternity in the hearts of men; yet they cannot fathom what God has done from beginning to end.
>
> Ecclesiastes 3:11 (NIV)

I have never trusted in God's timing before, and this was one time where I was still questioning him and how he could let this happen, so trusting him on his timing was hard. However, I praised him for letting Brady go home when he was ready and not allowing my plan be the way. My plans don't always turn out very well and may not always be the best idea. Several times throughout this documented journey, being a Christian wasn't always easy for me, so my walk with Christ was on rocky road most of the time. I was too busy living for material things, chasing money, and wanting more when, in reality, all I needed was above me, watching over me, God. I had already accepted Jesus but just was not living for him. Beth and I tried to find a church, but our hearts must have not been in it with us because we could find plenty excuses for not attending. After working all week, maybe some late nights, I wanted the weekend for myself. I would go ride my motorcycle at Watkins or Thunder Valley. I was living for Tommy, not God. Is this why Brady had a stroke so I would lean more on God? Was it to ground me and refocus my priorities? Or was this God's plan for Brady all along? What is it? I have wondered about this for so long. As life unfolds, there are times when I would say to myself, "Self, this might just be the reason." Or I would say, "Self, don't miss the next time God comes calling or knocking because next time, the result might be worse."

As we continued to prepare for our move back home, Brady was still working hard in rehab and leaving lasting impressions with his nurses, therapists, and doctors. Brady met another young boy the week before being discharged. This young boy also suffered a stroke. He was in town participating in a baseball tournament. Apparently, something caused his blood pressure to shoot way up, *boom*, and stroke occurred. I am not sure how his story ended, but we did go back several times to visit with his parents. While we would visit with them, I would get the little belly pain people get when they are feeling very attached to the person sharing a story. When we would go back to Children's Hospital, Brady would visit the nurses' station to show off what he had achieved in rehab. They were always so amazed at how far he had come since June 10. It was important to him, at age nine, to let them know how much he appreciated them caring for him all those days.

Dr. Miller made some rounds during Brady's last week there. He was excited at how much he had made over the five weeks since meeting Brady. He assured us he would be seeing Brady again in a few months but told us to focus on the rehab because it was the most important to his continued recovery.

Going home was stressful. As his parents, we were becoming the main caregivers, but really Beth was going to because I needed to get back to work. I had been away for five weeks. Even though I returned to work part-time at first, Brady's day-to-day care was all on her. On the outside, she was taking care of things like nothing was ever wrong, but on the inside, I know she was crushed.

We lived in a small 1,900-square-foot two-story home with all the bedrooms on the second floor. Actually, our bedroom was up about three steps from the second floor. Navigating the stairs in the house would prove to be a challenge, but Brady proved us wrong again. After only a short time, he was showing us he could do it. Another concern was since our room was not exactly next door to his, would we hear him try to get up at night to go to the restroom? If we didn't, then would he be at risk?

In addition to Brady going home, Will was finally coming home from Tennessee. Mary and Will arrived on July 19. Finally, I had everyone back together and at home. I hadn't seen Will in about three weeks. Excitement was all over Brady's face when we told him his little brother would be home.

Over the last few days in the hospital, we began to meet with Brady's therapists to learn what we needed to focus on when we took Brady home. They gave us a few cue cards to work on memory recall and speech as well as many exercises to keep Brady moving the best we could. As July 15 came closer, his blood levels weren't cooperating, so the doctor was talking like they should keep him longer. In the end, the doctors knew it was time for Brady to return home and start his new life adapting and making necessary changes so he could function at home. Walking out of that hospital was bittersweet. Those people cared not only for Brady but for Beth and me too. We formed new friendships with people who have given their life to care for others.

I remember posting "We are Home! We are Home!" on Brady's care page that afternoon. As we pulled up to the house, we noticed someone had made a sign and posted it in the yard. It read, "Welcome home, Brady," and of course, it came from the neighbors. Bringing him home was more special than the day he was born. We were all overcome with emotion. I can only imagine what was going through his mind. He had not seen his room or the dogs in such a long time.

Those darn neighbors of ours really put the homecoming over the top with the yard sign. For everything they did for us, they never asked for anything in return and never complained about doing whatever we needed. They have no idea how special they are to me for everything they did for us and Brady. After all, they treated Brady like one their own. Social media is one of many ways to keep in touch with distant friends and family. Brady recently posted something on Facebook, and this was a reply:

Brady, you are such an inspiration! I can still remember that day like it was yesterday. There were so many people praying for you, for healing, for strength, for patience. God had a plan for you and your family. Look at you now, my gosh, you have adapted and conquered! The world is yours! XO.

—Posted on Tommy Jones's Facebook by
Judy Lance on July 20, 2013

That is very special and shows the type of people I am talking about when I mentioned the neighbors.

Five weeks ago, Brady was leaving for school to see his friends and wrap up the second grade. Now he was returning home a changed person facing many challenges. He left walking, talking, playful, smiling, and doing things on his own. He was riding his bike, skateboard, and was wanting a motorcycle. When he came home on July 15, 2005, he was barely able to walk, could only speak about ten words, and forgot riding anything. The severity of Brady's condition was he went back to being a newborn but in a nine-year-old body.

During the five weeks at the hospital, he improved more than anyone could have dreamed, but he was nowhere close to being ready to go back to school or even being able to do the simple tasks like button his pants, ties his shoes, or bathe himself.

On our way home, Brady wanted to eat at Red Lobster, so we stopped at the place located in Park Meadows near our house. Lunch was very good, and Brady ate everything he could get on his plate. He was still learning to be left-handed, so eating wasn't the easiest, but Mommy and Daddy made sure he enjoyed his lunch. Gil, the manager, knew us from our more than several nights eating there. He happened to be on duty that afternoon, so he approached us as he normally would. When we opened up about Brady's condition, he was in shock. He decided to buy Brady's lunch for us to show he cared. Again, the small acts of kindness make a difference in attitude and really mean something to me. Acts of kindness are never ending and get me emotional every time I witness someone doing something like this; even today, thinking about it makes me have watery eyes.

Beth and I realized all the things people had done for us after being home. Some people did the yard work, cleaned, and took care of the dogs. Oh man, were they happy to see Brady; equally, he was excited to see them. After being gone for so long, we realized there was more to be done to prepare for being home with him, so I was hoping he would rest some so Beth and I could get something off the "to do" list. He still didn't have much endurance since he needed to rely heavily on his left side. He got worn out pretty quickly. We had to deal with the opposite too. There were times when Brady would just get up and start walking somewhere. He wouldn't know why or where he was going, but he wanted up. We witnessed it several times in the hospital. The doctors said this should go away over time as he got better.

We had a special note waiting for us when we got home. Someone from the Makita Suzuki Motocross team invited us to be their guests at the upcoming outdoor national race. The race was the following weekend, so we would have to watch the head and the length of the day. Most people don't think of Denver getting warm, but in the summer, it can get pretty hot. Denver isn't always under snow, even in the winter, the snow usually melts as fast as it comes down, especially if you are facing south.

At the race, we got to tour a few larger team race trucks, get close to the race bikes, and meet some really cool people. Brady grew up around semi-trucks because Larry had been in business for many years hauling cargo all over. When we would visit Memphis, Brady loved going to Gramps' office because he might get to sit in a big truck. In addition to the race, we were also invited to an autograph signing to be held the night before the race at a local motorcycle dealership.

The week ahead became a real test as I returned to work part-time: Brady started his outpatient rehab with new therapists, Will came home, and there were other activities. One day, we decided to take Brady swimming to see what he could do. In a mere minute, he was swimming. Mr. Johnson came by one day so Beth and I could run some errands, and Brady began playing his PlayStation. He was getting the right hand involved to play as best as possible. Brady was determined to play his games.

A Great Kid

I t was time for our motocross weekend to start. Friday, we went to Faye Myers to attend an autograph session with Team Makita Suzuki. We saw our friend who we had met back in June when we were teaching Brady how to ride a dirt bike before his stroke. It's too bad this time we wouldn't be setting up the next time to go riding. We stood around and talked to the Oakley representatives, sales people from the dealership, and other people we knew.

As Brady went up to get autographs from the team riders, we met one of the 250 class riders. He was so young but showed an interest in Brady because he knew someone in their early 40s who recently suffered a stroke. I am not sure he expected the relationship to continue over the next eight years and beyond, but it has.

We arrived at the race track on Saturday morning and walked around the pit area. This is a place where all the riders have their transportation vehicles set up with parts, mechanics, and hospitality tents. It's a place where the fans have the opportunity to get close to the riders for autographs and conversation. Brady really didn't want to use the wheelchair, so he walked quite a bit on the uneven terrain of the mountainside. We finally found the Team Suzuki area, and as we were approaching, we saw the rider from the night before. He invited us to have a seat under the team's tent, offered us drinks, and told us to relax. This was a very polite sixteen-year-old kid who was befriending a family he hardly knew. Why was he being so nice? I don't know; maybe I should ask him the next time I talk to him. As we sat there for hours, he would check on Brady from time to time. We would walk around some and come back so we could get Brady out of the sun. At different times, we got pictures of the young rider and Brady. The team also gave us a team hat, which the three riders autographed for us. That hat still hangs in our movie room.

During the day, we got to see other riders and their trucks. We also met the famous number 4 rider from Florida, the team manager, and the team trainer. We took advantage of talking with the team trainer to get his perspective on what Brady was going through. He offered his advice but told us we were doing the right things by getting Brady out and giving him some unofficial physical therapy. I decided it had been long day after the first practice, so we packed up and headed for home. Brady kept talking about how much fun he had, so I knew I was locked in to taking back the next day. Back then, the outdoor races took place over two days, with practice one day and the races the next.

On day 2, Brady couldn't muster the energy to walk, so he rode the entire time in his wheelchair, except for the times we would sit at the Suzuki tent and rest.

The young rider has continued to be a friend to us and someone Brady looks up to. I don't think he realizes it to the extent, but every time there is a race on TV, Brady will ask where he is or how he is doing. We had the opportunity to see him in Atlanta several times, and we even drove to Jacksonville, Florida, to see him in 2012. Brady still gets a little nervous to talk with him, plus I don't think he knows what to say to someone who has become sort of a celebrity.

Like I said, I am not sure the young man realizes what the time he gave meant to Brady, and even me. Seeing someone go out of their way to put a smile on a little boy's face is such an uplifting thing to watch. He didn't have to do this. There wasn't anyone standing around telling him this is good PR or that he needed to be kind to kids. Was God present that day at Thunder Valley? Did God have a hand in this starting relationship? Things don't just happen; they happen for a reason. I still stay in contact today and usually text him every Saturday morning during the season to offer my two cents' worth of encouragement and motivation. He doesn't need me doing this. He has a whole team behind him, but it is a small way to repay him for what he did eight years ago.

> For it is God who works in you to will and to act according to his good purpose.
>
> Philippians 2:13 (NIV)

Was this young man doing this on his own? I don't believe he acted alone as there is a God who presented the path for him. I hope Brady's story will be something he cherishes and remembers as his own son grows up.

He has a lot to learn from his father. Now, at the age of twenty-four, he has suffered some setbacks in life, but he overcomes just like Brady. They have more in common than they both realize. I pray Brady has the opportunity to spend a little time with him some day to thank him for being such an inspiration. The young man is none other than #18, Davi Millsaps. We are behind you!

Now What?

Well, August 1 marked the first time the whole family was back together and all alone. Mary needed to get back to her regular routine. The last seven weeks had been trying on her also. She doesn't know this, but she was a big rock for me when she came back with Will. I am not sure how most people view their relationship with their in-laws, but I cherish mine and have learned I can tell my mother-in-law almost anything. Our relationship started a little differently than most. Three months after being married to her daughter, I had to have hernia surgery. Beth worked for her dad, so she stayed home a few days, but she needed to get back to do payroll and other things, so Mary came over to sit with me. I was twenty-two years old, so you could say young and full of myself. Part of caring for me was having to assist me to the bathroom with some help sometimes. This will pretty much make any relationship last because neither really want to talk about it afterward. She was very helpful then, and she still is today. Thanks, Mom.

Since we were all alone now, it was time to get life on a structured path somehow. School was going to be starting, but we learned that school wasn't ready for Brady. They didn't have the right people in place to assist him throughout his day because they really had no idea as to the extent of his injuries. The school kept saying to bring him and they would make sure he was in the right place and make sure he learned. I thought there was more to it than that, so I called a meeting with the school administrators. I had to inform them of Brady's condition and let them know he would need full-time assistance. He would need assistance going to the bathroom, walking, and carrying books, his backpack and his lunch tray. They had the notion his disabilities were only physical and forgot about the learning problems he had due to the large amount of brain damage. Most people assume when someone has a stroke, their limitations are only physical, and that is the furthest from the truth. This is the same people who had to make sure I knew the situation was handled by the guidelines for emergencies with the school. At the meeting, Beth and I were emotional as I expected. Plus, it is hard to not hurt someone's feelings in a situation like that because you know you are sending your child back to the place where the last time he was there, he passed out and did not walk out on his own. We learned the school had received approval to hire Brady his own assistant or para-pro. Since there was still more details to work out, Brady wasn't able to start on time with his friends. We all understood, but Brady didn't. He just wanted to be with his friends. I was hoping he would start because with boys in school, Beth would be able to get a much-needed break from this situation for several hours a day. Since she was around Brady the most, I could see it when I got home from work; she was worn down physically and emotionally. My heart broke for her because she never got to get away from it unless the weekend was free from other responsibilities. To this day, I don't think I have ever told her what she meant to me during this time. I thought I was being her rock, and I think she ended up being mine by taking most of the burden from Brady's outpatient rehab and continued recovery. I did go to the blood draws when they were needed, because Brady asked me to. I guess I was his rock when giving blood.

Before Brady went back to school, we made our TV debut on a PBS show, *Keeping Kids Healthy*. They sent a producer and film crew to our house to do the episode that focused on pediatric strokes and Brady's story. There was a school picnic scheduled, so we went there first with the film crew. They interviewed Mr. Johnson as well as got some great footage of Brady walking with his friend, Miller. Afterward, they came back to the house to set up a more serious interview with Beth and me. It was hard to make it through without balling, but we held it together. There were several topics discussed, but our main thing was the need for more awareness about pediatric strokes. Considering the ER doctors had no clue or even how to treat it, there was a major time lapse, which created most of the damage for Brady. Now there is no guarantee in life, so if the doctors had known something and been able to treat him, who knows what the outcome would have been. However, if we knew about strokes in children, we might have asked if he was having a stroke and what could be done to test for it.

Over the five weeks in the hospital and several weeks after being home, we noticed our frustration level with the ER doctors and team was still real pain for us, so we decided to seek council. Even though there was nothing council could do for Brady, I still wanted answers from the hospital, so I had a meeting with the main ER doctor and a director of the hospital. On that day in June, the ER doctor found it more important to go home for dinner than to help find out what was going on with Brady. She even told us she was leaving to go make dinner for her family. Why was Brady's care not her top priority? Was this an hourly employee who would be over in hours and collect overtime or something? Most of the time, while in the ER, we saw the nurses and not her. It's like she didn't care or didn't have the proper training to care for him, so she sort of ignored it.

During the meeting, I cried. I lost my temper, and I drilled the doctors about everything that day. I wanted her to feel my pain as a parent. The director of the hospital kept the meeting very cordial and moved for some kind of closure. Brady didn't pass away, but the pain I felt then was as real as losing him. The ER doctor mentioned she would really like to see Brady, but I never took him up there to see her. Time went on, and I now understand a little better about the ER and how things work. I hope she has learned from that day; I know I have.

To help spread the awareness, Mr. Johnson organized the Strokes for Strokes Golf Tournament at Links Golf Course in Highlands Ranch, Colorado. He asked me to help get some sponsors, so I called several golf manufacturers. None of them were interested in the cause or willing to donate anything for the tournament until, finally, I got in touch with Tracey Flowers from Callaway Golf. When I explained the situation, she was mortified to hear it and was willing to help in any way. She sent us over two hundred golf balls, golf towels, and hats. Everyone who entered received a little package thanks to Callaway Golf. Ogio donated a few golf bags, and Oakley gave us several pairs of sunglasses. There were others who stepped up to help also by donating weekend getaways and other great items. Mr. Johnson scheduled the event for October 1, 2005. Now it was time to get players to attend.

By now, we had done several interviews and articles for the local papers to help spread the awareness about pediatric stroke. One of the headlines read, "9-year-old boy slowly recovers from stroke." Another article title read, "Stroke strikes 9-year-old boy." I was on a crusade to spread the word somehow. I quickly realized, since I was not someone of position and Brady was just an everyday kid, there wasn't many people who wanted to get behind any awareness campaign. This was very disheartening to me, considering a stroke can happen to any child, healthy or not. Six in one hundred thousand children will suffer a stroke, and 12 percent of those will die from the stroke. [from, www.CHASA.org] Maybe it is a small amount, but our kids are the future, so someone needed to spread the word. I even tried to get someone to do a public service announcement, but there was never any takers, so guess what? I pretty much gave up.

During all this time, Brady was continuing to rehabilitate at the outpatient center. He was doing well, but there were very small strides. It really seemed like he hit a wall and wasn't making as many improvements as he did while in the hospital. It wasn't because of his lack of trying. He tried; he pushed, and he even got mad. He wanted to see the improvements. His speech was making the biggest gains. As the brain recovered, his speech and recall center would respond more than the physical parts.

The school was finally ready for him to attend school, so August 9, 2005, was his first day back at school. When we told him he was ready, he began to cry. He was scared, but he was shedding happy tears. He knew it had been a long road to get here, and he was ready. Even though he only attended half days at first, he didn't care. He was heading back to school, and he would be reunited with his friends. Brady got tired pretty easy, so it was good to have him only go half days for a while to build his endurance.

Family and Friends Matter

My brother Troy and I decided we would put together a motocross fund-raiser to raise money for Brady's recovery and to spread the awareness. We chose a track outside of Brandon, Florida, named Bartow MX. I had many contacts within the industry from the last time I was involved in a motocross fund-raiser. He came to Denver for work, and we started planning it all out. I was able to get a few announcements about the event and the cause in the national motocross magazines. Hence, the Cause2Ride Foundation was created. We chose CHASA, Children's Hemiplegia and Stroke Association, as the benefactor for the proceeds from the event.

Troy's visit was the first time he had seen Brady since his stroke. Today, I am not sure what he thought or how he processed it, considering he has three girls of his own. I believe he was a little shocked because until you see Brady and spend time with him, it's hard to understand the true challenges he faces. My brother and I have not always been close, and even today, we seem to drift apart for some reason. I am sure we are no different than other siblings out there. I am not sure where we got off with our relationship. Maybe I wronged him along the way, or maybe he wronged me. I do know this—he will always be my brother. Over time since Brady's stroke, I have change my views and learned to love my brother as God teaches us in 1 Peter.

> Now that you have purified yourselves by obeying the truth so that you have sincere love for your brothers, love one another deeply, from the heart.
>
> 1 Peter 1:22 (NIV)

> This is how my heavenly Father will treat each of you unless you forgive your brother from the heart.
>
> Matthew 18:35 (NIV)

When I was young, I called my brother "Froy" because I couldn't pronounce the "tr" combination very well. Just as I am doing, I ask everyone to think about their relationship with their brothers or sisters and really think about the scripture. Are you loving your brother from the heart? Have you forgiven your brother for some past mistakes he made? When was the last time you told him you loved him or how you felt about them? For me, I recently did, but he deserves to hear it more often. "Troy, I love you for all you do and are. We don't see eye to eye all the time, and I am sure somewhere, we broke Mom's heart for drifting apart, but I hope that changes, forever moving forward. I need you to be a part of my life." As hard as it is to write that for the world to see, it shows the admiration I have for him.

I have written about Mr. Johnson and the great neighbors already, but enough can't be said about them. We were given the opportunity to take a Saturday and Saturday night away from home because Mr. Johnson and the Lance family watched the boys and dogs for us. The endless selflessness these people have shown us is just immeasurable. While Beth and I were away, Brady had a little accident at the park where he skinned his chin and knee, but it was nothing major. He was trying to ride his scooter and just fell over. When we returned home, he was quiet. Later, he said he missed us, plus the fall scared him. It will take awhile for him to get over that fear. After he learned to keep his balance, he was able to move much faster and even avoid falls.

Beth also has a brother. His name is Brad Phillips. He announced he would be coming to visit us about a month after Troy was with us. It was great to have both of them visit so soon. Brad's visit was good for Beth and me. While he was visiting, we took the boys to the park, but we had another scare. I was teaching Will how to ride his bike without training wheels, and we played touch football. Will accidentally tripped into Brady while trying to tag him, and they both fell to the ground. Brady hit his right side of his head pretty hard on the grass. He cried for almost five minutes and then was very emotional for a while afterward. I wasn't close enough to catch him, but I saw the look on his face, and he was terrified since he had no way to catch himself on the right side. He wanted to do so many things and struggled just to do the simple things. Brady had to adjust to a new way of life. I was praying a lot back then that this would be the worst thing he would endure. I can't promise him this will be the worst. He has fought so hard to overcome his stroke for eight years. What he doesn't know is that he is my motivation to keep me moving and trying my hardest to accomplish things. He will realize some day that he is the reason our family is so close and strong.

Since Brad was visiting, I was able to focus on work since he was with Beth and the boys. My wife took Brady's stroke very hard, so when we had the chance to get help, it made me feel a little better since I knew she was getting help and not having to do things by herself. Brad took care of the boys a few days so Beth could get some much-needed rest. He did some "brotherly dos" around the house for us. We stayed up late playing Xbox, eating, and just talking. We even went to the driving range to hit some golf balls. Neither of us were very good back then, so it was a crazy feat to hit golf balls. Over the years, we have both improved our golf game, and I try to play very regularly. At the end of his visit, I found his trip to be more helpful for me than I imagined.

Family and friends are an important part of everyone's daily lives. Everyone needs and deserves to have that special someone to lean on during hard times, celebrate with during good times, and to share a meal. If you were granted this from God, don't ever take it for granted. Call them as much as you can. Give them a hug when you see them, or even send them a little hand-written note. E-mails have lost the personal touch, so send something with emotion. I am not talking about the cute little icons on text. Everyone likes to get surprises from people who care about us. If getting a nice message or note from someone puts a smile on your face, return the favor. Be the first to send a note to them next time. If you like hearing their voice, call them. If you cherish their friendship, then tell them.

> So in everything, do to others what you would
> have them do to you, for this sums up the Law
> and the Prophets.
>
> Matthew 7:12 (NIV)

Continued Adjusting

B rady had settled into a routine with school and was continuing his rehab. However, he hit a plateau several months after leaving the hospital. Dr. Miller said he would hit these at times but should stay focused so he could push through them to next part of recovery. Brady had so many rehab appointments, so when he hit a plateau, it was a scary moment. I would ask myself, was he going to keep recovering, or did he finish? We decided to take him back to the doctor to see what was going on with him. I was not ready to hear he was done with recovery because he was so far away from full recovery. By this time, it had been about three and a half months since the stroke, and although we weren't ten to twelve months down the road, the outpatient rehab therapists started talking like this would be all he may ever get back. They even started talking about cutting his rehab back since they weren't seeing much improvement over a set period of time. Praise the Lord because he kept going as scheduled and made it through the plateau and began to improve more.

We did have the golf tournament to get us excited though. October 1, 2005, was the day for the tourney, and everyone was ready to play. We ended up with forty-eight players, and through various donations minus the tournament expenses, we raised over two thousand dollars to be used for Brady's recovery. Mr. Johnson really went above and beyond to make this tournament a success. I tried to fight back the tears, but there were forty-seven other people who shared in my passion by showing support for Brady. They paid money to the cause. It was humbling. Although my team placed fifth with a five under par, we were all winners on that day since we all came together for a common goal. Sometimes in life, you just want to give up on certain things. When tragedy strikes, your faith is tested. Beth and I had been tested for sure with Brady's stroke. We know we are on borrowed time from God, and the same goes for our kids. It was so easy to talk about how we were feeling or coping, but Brady was the true hero in this. He suffered a massive stroke, yet every day, he continued to pick up his chin, go to school, and struggle to learn, to play his games, and to talk.

We were approaching the six-month mark, and his ankle still hadn't moved. He was getting tired of wearing his leg brace and didn't want it anymore. This was a sad day for me, because I saw my son finally give up. He was mad. He was sad. He was very frustrated with it all. Even though he had been removed from his blood thinners, Dr. Miller thought he might still need something, so he put him on a stimulant medicine to slow the brain function down to see if Brady could focus better on learning and not lose attention so quickly. He had begun to stay at school for longer periods of time, which was good since he wasn't getting math for the first few months he was back at school; he had been leaving before that class started.

Somewhere around this time, the entire family got sick, and it hung around for almost three weeks. I ended up with strep throat, while Beth and Will had the dreaded stomach bug pay them a visit. Not to mention Beth had to have several moles removed, so she was sporting a few stitches in her shoulder. Brady was even still nursing his finger, which was slammed in a bathroom door at a restaurant several months prior; all the while, he had a sore on his foot that wouldn't go away. Eventually, we all got better, and Brady's foot and finger healed. During all this time, we received word our sister-in-law was pregnant with twins but had been placed on bed rest for a long time. I mean 2005 was a heck of a year for the Jones and Phillips families.

Thanksgiving was coming up, so Beth and I decided we would drive the boys to Memphis for the holidays. This was the first long car ride for Brady, so we were a little nervous. It was great to see the family get a little break. The parents really helped with Brady's needs, so Beth and I were able to breathe a little and get some much-needed rest. When we returned from our trip, we started planning for Christmas. Beth loves to decorate, and Christmas is no exception. She turns our house into a winter wonderland. It always looks and smells so nice but what a huge mess to clean up.

Our decorating was cut very short though. I had decided to leave the firm I was working with to focus on the family and possibly start my own firm. December 2, 2005, was supposed to be my last day, but the day before,

I received another panicked phone call. This time, it was from a neighbor who I had never met. He was telling me my family was being rushed to Swedish Medical Center. There were two gurneys removed from the house with people on them. I guess Beth had given him my number to inform me of what was going on at the house. Brady had fallen down the stairs and was knocked out, so Beth had to call 911. When the paramedics arrived, Brady was conscious, but they thought it was in his best interest to go ahead to the ER to be checked out. While the paramedics were attending to Brady, Will got locked knees and fainted at the site of Brady's blood when they gave him the IV. When the paramedics witnessed this, they thought Will was having a seizure. By this time, the police and fire department had shown up to go through our house to make sure there wasn't something in the house leaking that caused both boys to get hurt.

Brady had a CT scan preformed at the ER, which showed a small bleed in his brain. Last time, it was clot, and this time it was a bleed. My little boy couldn't catch a break. The ER doctor encouraged us to have Brady transferred to Children's since they were experts with kids. Obviously, Beth and I were okay with this since we lived there with Brady before. On the other bed was Will. The ER doctor was going to run some test on him, but by the time he decided to do them, Will was jumping on the bed and playing like nothing happened. The doctor chalked it up to simply fainting at the site of blood. Children's Hospital was our next stop via the ambulance. Since Beth rode with Brady before, I got to ride this time. Actually, Beth was getting Will to our great neighbors so they could watch him since we had no idea what was going on with Brady.

Once we got to the hospital, they admitted him to the PICU (pediatric intensive care unit). The next thirty hours was like living in a twilight zone. One doctor wanted to do brain surgery and another wanted to do some invasive testing. The one who wanted to perform brain surgery thought Brady's vessels were weak, and that is what caused the bleed, which in turn can cause the stroke. You have got to be kidding me. He had another stroke just six months after the other one? Really? Thank God for Dr. Miller. He finally made it from vacation to the hospital to tell us Brady was fine and probably lost his balance and fell down the stairs. The fall caused the small bleed in the brain. He saw no signs of a stroke. This was the most expensive thirty hours. Since he had a bleed, they had to watch him in the PICU instead of a regular room. The entire time, Brady was playing video games and eating some pretty good food; I don't recall him really sleeping either. He wanted to leave and wasn't acting like there was nothing wrong, so we got him transferred to the fifth floor again. Some doctors can be very over-the-top thinkers. I am sorry, but if it hadn't been for Dr. Miller, my little boy would have been going to the OR for brain surgery. About thirty hours later, Brady was sent home.

We were back to preparing for Christmas. Brady took a break from rehab over the Christmas holidays, which was nice for all of us because we got to hang out together and not worry about the appointments. Brady and Will were getting so excited the closer we got to Christmas morning. There was a birthday party for a neighbor, so we all went to Monkey Business, an indoor facility with inflatable bouncing areas to play. Brady did pretty well except for mingling with others. Some of the kids stared at him and made him feel uncomfortable; however, when I played with him, he did great on the obstacles. He even pulled himself up the rope ladder with steps. His left arm was getting so much use it had begun to show signs of a bodybuilder. He continues to show off that physique and mental strength.

We all had a wonderful Christmas. We spent Christmas Eve with the Stantons and Christmas Day with the Lance family. We even went to the movies. Somewhere during the break, we noticed the stimulant meds Brady was taking were causing him to zone out way too much, so we decided to speak with Dr. Miller about taking him off. He agreed we would take him off. Once we took him off the meds, Brady seemed to be more alert and actually a bit happier.

New Beginnings

Christmas has come and gone but the memoires of this year will be with me forever. As I struggle to write this update due to emotions, I reflect on 2005. Beth and I along with our families will never forget this year. It started in February and went until December with many challenging things to overcome. However, 2005 is ending on a high note for the Jones and Phillips families. Any day now, we are expecting to an aunt and uncle again. Brad and his wife, Kristen are expecting twins. In addition Beth and I got the news we have been waiting to share. We will be relocating to Atlanta, GA next month. We are so excited to be starting a new job and being only 6 hours from our parents. At the same time, it will be hard to leave behind the great people of Denver. This is a move that we feel, as a family, is better for everyone. It is a great career opportunity for me, yet at the same time, puts us very close to our family. Brady and Will are excited to be closer to their grandparents. We are interviewing schools the first of the month to see where Brady will best suited. We also have started looking for a place to live, but are holding out as long as we can to decide until we have the school location nailed down. We are hoping to make the move seamless for the kids.

—Posted by Tommy Jones on
Brady Jones's care page on December 28, 2005

"For I know the plans I have for you," declares the Lord, "plans to prosper you and not harm you, plans to give you hope and a future."

Jeremiah 29:11 (NIV)

This is so true, isn't it? The Lord knows what he wants for us; we just have to lean into him and see what his plans are. We also need to be willing to embrace them.

During his recovery, I took a job offer in Atlanta, Georgia. My posts explains why this was a good move for us, and it wasn't like we hadn't moved across the country before. In 1998, we left Memphis for Denver. In 2003, we left Denver for Tampa, Florida, which Beth calls our extended vacation. At the beginning of 2004, we left Tampa for Denver again. I didn't want to bounce from job to job, but things happened, which caused us to move. In 2003, I had my own firm, and due to 9-11, it took a huge hit, so we needed to find a job back in the public practice, and Florida finally came up, so we took it. In December of 2003, I was laid off from that company, so I called the firm in Denver where I had interviewed prior to moving to Tampa. They offered me a job, so we went to Denver for our second stay. Due to Brady's stroke, I decided to leave that firm in December 2005, but the job in Atlanta came my way, so there is a short history lesson and about three boring minutes of your life that you will not get back.

I went to work as a designer with a national home builder. I really interviewed for a project manager position, but until the family got moved out, my new boss thought it would be best to bring me in as a designer first. This way, I would have a bit more flexibility with my schedule. I began interviewing schools for Brady where we thought we needed to live. We ended up in Forsyth County in the small but over populated city of Cumming, Georgia. This was about twenty-two miles north of my new office, but the school we decided was best for Brady was located only about four miles from the house. So less than three weeks later, the family moved to a rental house in a brand-new community. The house had never been lived in, and the master bedroom was on the first floor. At first, we were concerned about being away from Brady in case he tried to come down the stairs in the middle of the night or something. The good thing about the stairs is they had a midlanding that turned, so if something happened to either of them, they wouldn't fall very far.

I had to get Brady's school and medical records together for the new school. The school was more than equipped to handle situations like ours, and the principal was very welcoming and understanding about Brady's condition. I asked to do a presentation with his teachers to prepare them for what they would be dealing with. Again, most people assumed his limitations were more physical when in reality, it was about 50-50 physical and mental learning. It took us a while to get both kids registered because we had to have so much more paperwork than I remember in Denver. Once that was all together, the boys started school. What an adjustment for them—not only did Will start going to school all day right away, but this school system wasn't on the track system like Denver, so they only had a few shorts months until the next grade. It wasn't long until Brady was making 100s on his spelling tests. That was huge accomplishment for him.

Brady did very well with his third grade and the transfer across the country. I was worried if I made the right decision, but he was fitting in very well. All the kids were very polite and friendly to Brady. He went from a school of about four hundred students to one with almost a thousand kids in the elementary school alone. He didn't seem to be overwhelmed. Since we moved, it meant finding a rehab facility for Brady and possibly a new neurologist. The rehab center was the easiest part, but the neurologist was complicated and frustrating. We called a doctor located in the medical area of Dunwoody. We took all of Brady's records and films to the appointment. The doctor talked to us and examined Brady for almost two hours. He acted very concerned about the limited recovery Brady had achieved. In his mind, Brady should have been further along to the point where he asked us how bad Brady was when he had the stroke. He said he wanted to review the films and he would make copies. He asked us to schedule a follow-up with him after we had evaluations done from the different therapists. However, when we went back, not only did I get to have a very unpleasant conversation with the lady at the counter, but we learned the doctor never reviewed Brady's records, and somewhere along the way, he misplaced Brady's films. This guy didn't do anything but lose films. We walked out and never looked back. Brady hasn't seen a neurologist since Dr. Miller in Denver. We did get him back into rehab two days a week through the Alpharetta location of Children's Healthcare of Atlanta. Brady seemed to like his new therapist team. I think as long as they are helping him, he would like a monkey.

The Atlanta Supercross race was coming up soon, and we got to be guests at the race. We went down to the pit area before the public could enter so Brady could check everything out before the mad crowd entered. We went by the Honda truck to see Davi Millsaps. While we were at the race, Brady ran into a kid from school. When the long day was over, he just kept saying how much fun he had, and it gave him a small connection with the kid from school. Shortly after the event, Mary and Larry came to Atlanta for their first visit. It allowed Beth and me to relax a bit. They ended up taking the kids back to Memphis for spring break, so we got to spend some much-needed quality time together.

Since we relocated to Atlanta, I was able to help my brother plan the Cause2Ride event, which was scheduled for March 19, 2006. Previously, I worked hard to spread the awareness about pediatric stroke. Between Troy and I, we were able to get some pro riders and freestyle team to attend the fund-raiser. Brady was excited so many people were coming to show their support and help raise money. The visit to Florida was going to be the first time Brady's cousins saw him since his stroke, so I was worried how they would respond, but I knew they would love him anyway. Since the ride was between Tampa and Orlando, we got to attend the Orlando Supercross race.

This time, we were guest of the promoter and even got to get on stage to announce the ride and talk about pediatric stroke. This helped get more people to come out for the ride, plus we were able to obtain several autographed jerseys from other riders for the auction the following day. The event was a success. We raised a lot of money for a great cause and had fun doing it. One jersey raised over seven hundred dollars from one woman. It just so happened Davi was in attendance to sign autographs and take pictures. At only seventeen years old, I don't think he could have thought his jersey would raise that kind of money. Again, it was for a great cause, and it helped spread the word to many people. No kid is exempt from a stroke.

Can Time Stop?

I woke up one day and thought to myself, *the last six months had flown by, and where does all the time go?* It was almost Brady's tenth birthday, which meant it was close to a year since his stroke. How was I going to deal with this day? How would Beth, Brady, and Will handle this day? At this time in my life, I still wasn't walking back with God, so I wasn't praying for peace. I wasn't surrendering the situation to him. I was walking alone. We had asked Brady if he wanted to try and play soccer because I had found several special needs programs I thought he might want to join. He turned them down and got really angry. I remember him saying he wanted to play football and ride a motorcycle. These were two things he was looking forward to doing just days before his stroke.

Brady's birthday came, and it was nice. He had a good day, then it was June 10, 2006, the one year anniversary. I cried almost all day. I am not typically one to cry like that. It was a very tough day for me. We wanted to treat it like any other day and asked for people to take a moment of silence to honor Brady and others like him. We also were informed the TV show we filmed back in July of the previous year would finally be airing on June 12–16. I couldn't watch it when it came on, and I still find it hard to watch it on YouTube.

On June 19, 2006, we had some great news from his therapists. They all were seeing signs of improvement, so it was time to strike while we could with more rehab. Now Brady had grown tired of being different and less functional than others. So I rigged his bike with a pedal to keep his right foot on it, and off he went for a short distance. He could ride it, but when he got nervous, his foot would still slip off, plus if something were to happen and he fell to the right, he wouldn't be able to put his leg out. He stayed interested for about one to two months and gave up. That was sad, considering he was finally moving, but he became very frustrated with it. When he would get stressed, his right arm would tighten up and draw up to his shoulder, so we later found out he was having trouble keeping his hand on the handle bars.

His physical therapist recommended an arm brace that looked like that of the terminator. This arm brace would keep tension on the right arm so it would stay in a folded position rather than up to his shoulder. I thought the brace would work, and I believe it did, but Brady refused to wear it out in public or to school. "It draws more attention, Dad," he would say. We understood, but we really pushed him to wear it. As he grew, though, the brace would need to change in size, which meant exchanging it for another one. We did this for several months up to close to a year, and Brady just said, "No more." He was finished with wearing the brace.

It was time for another break, so Brady and Will went back to Memphis for two weeks this time. Beth and I got a chance to see some of Atlanta without the little ones. This was coming at a good time because school was going to be starting soon. Before they left, we got a call from the National Stroke Association. They had heard about Brady's story and featured him as the "champion of hope" in their September issue. Brady was really excited and hoped the magazine reached a lot of people.

All this time flew by, and it was looking like it wasn't slowing down. School was about to start; I had received a promotion to project manager, and Will was going to try his luck at soccer in the fall. I really fell into a pattern of neglect. I focused more on my work and not so much on home. I had an outlet of sorts. I got to go to work, and by this time, I was doing some light traveling. Beth never got a break unless the kids were gone to visit family. I can only imagine what she thought of me during this time. I even put my own desires before hers. It had been a long time since I rode my dirt bike, so I started doing it again. One day here and one day there turned into almost an every weekend thing. At times, I would think about her and wondered how much longer it would be before she left. I wasn't trying to run her off, but I found myself needing time to do my things, and I didn't consider her. God showed me this in 2007, when I crashed my motocross bike while preparing for an uphill sixty foot jump. My back tire slid out before the takeoff, and I flew about sixty-five feet before hitting the ground. I cracked my helmet since I hit the ground so hard. I also broke ribs, my leg, and suffered a concussion. Even though God gave me a sign it was time to start living for him and put my attention toward my family, it still hurt like hell. He could have helped with the painful crash, but this was his way. It took me several months to heal from that crash. During my healing time, I didn't miss but one day of work, and I never let Beth know how bad I was hurt. Riding my dirt bike was not something she accepted. She would tell me, "If you get hurt, I am going to kill you! We don't have the money for you to get hurt and not work or can't afford the medical bills." So even if I was hurt, I tried to hide it the best I could so I would not feel her wrath. The day after the accident, I pulled myself up, and I went to a home show with her. We had been planning this for months. I knew I was in bad shape because every time I stood up from sitting, there was so much pain in my leg I wanted to cry. I have to admit, the crash, seeing how I still don't remember much about it, did me in and helped me get back on the right path. Again, time doesn't stop, and I had to push through it.

> Husbands, love your wives, just as Christ loved the church and gave himself up for her.
>
> Ephesians 5:25 (NIV)

I feel like I have missed so many years with my wife because I strayed from God. Time doesn't stop to correct the wrongdoings. There is no pause button or rewind. There is no backspace in life. If I was married to myself, then I would have kicked myself to the curb. As I look back at this time in my life, I was an absent father and husband. I tried to always be there for Brady, but was I there for Will or Beth? Can I get a rewind and see if I was and if not, correct it? No, life doesn't work that way. At the same time, she was struggling with the move to Atlanta and the separation from a few good friends. One had moved to Seattle just before Brady's stroke, and the other one was still in Denver, but we moved. Shortly after we moved, we found out the friend in Denver was getting a divorce. Things back in Denver weren't the same anymore, and I tried telling her that, but she needed me to lend a shoulder and a hug, not try to fix her. I still struggle with this today, and I think most men do. Most of us are doers and want things fixed so we can move on to the next thing. As bad as it sounds, I think sometimes, men view women as the next thing. I do admit that, while coping, I did. We don't have good bedside manners or compassion when needed it most. Half the time, we don't think with the correct anatomy, and we become wrapped up in what makes us happy that we forget about our wives' needs. So maybe we should stop time to think more about them before our own self-interest. I am still guilty of this today to an extent, albeit not near as bad as I was before. I should be in bed with her right now, considering it is the wee hours of the morning.

Over The Years

How many of us remember our elementary and middle school years? I do remember some of mine. I was a BMX racer and a baseball player in Texas, and I started to find girls of interest. School was okay, but I seem to remember more of my time away from school. However, I will always remember Brady's transitions into school. He transitioned from elementary school in Highlands Ranch to Vickery Creek in Cumming, Georgia. He transitioned from the elementary school to Vickery Creek Middle School and then on to West Forsyth High School. Why will this stick with me? I had to prepare a presentation of every transition point to give his teachers and educators an insight to how he was before them and how he was at the time he entered their school.

One time, I had to go back to the school because a teacher had put a very large *F* on an assignment Brady turned in to her, which is okay if he made the grade. Come to find out, the teacher wasn't up to date on his IEP that was in place, which allowed him extra time to complete the task. An IEP stands for individualized education plan and is typically used for those with any type of disability or learning disorder. Brady's IEP had been put together by his therapists and teachers in Denver. They knew what he needed. So when we transferred him to Georgia, it took some teachers by surprise. Why some of them wouldn't take the time to read it is beyond me. They assumed they knew, and that is okay too. I just needed to educate them. This was the same thing when he went to middle school. Not only did he have an IEP in place, but he was placed in co-taught classes as much as possible. He had a male para-pro he could rely on if he needed help with the restrooms. This person also helped him navigate the halls during the day.

His two and a half years of elementary school was pretty quiet except for one incident. Brady had been very quiet about his school days for a few weeks. We would ask him how his day was and if anything happened that we needed to know about. The answer was always no until one day, he decided to open up. There was another kid who had been picking on him about his walking and running. He was telling Brady he couldn't run fast and was slow. When I heard this, I couldn't decide if I was upset emotionally or mad. I called the school the next morning and spoke with the principal. I filled her in on the situation and asked her to look into it. This type of situation is very sensitive, considering the boy could retaliate against Brady and do harm to him. Later that day, I received a call from the school, and the kid involved kindly apologized to me. I explained to him why his actions were hurtful. The school also called his parents. Several days later, I received another phone call. This time it was from the kid's parents. They were apologizing and inviting Brady to their house to spend some time with the other kid. I wasn't sure at first, but Brady wanted to go. Everything was fine after that time. School can be scary for our kids because all different things we hear happen there.

When Brady made his transition to middle school, we had to attend a day-long open house for parents and students. One of the speakers in attendance informed us that boys will be boys and the occasional scuffle may break out and other people standing around may accidentally get pushed or hit. This was a red flag, considering Brady couldn't afford to fall or take a hit to the head. Needless to say, I think he got caught up in one situation and he tripped, but he had learned how to roll to his good side for protection. He wasn't hurt or injured. As a matter of fact, the school didn't inform us of the situation; Brady did.

Another speaker we listened to spoke about the rules concerning public display of affection while at school. I guess they have had some hugs get carried away, so the school didn't allow it. That was fine with me. I was trying to keep Brady focused on school and not girls. They told us it was mainly a concern with the eighth graders and not so much with the incoming sixth graders. Brady was growing up, and this was the part of life I wasn't looking forward to. Brady, girls, school—man, it was a lot of changes at once.

Brady started showing interest in music, so we encouraged him to sign up for chorus. During his middle school years, he did chorus all three years. He has some talent, come to find out. He was involved in a few short solo acts and short duets. He also was a member of a

Ragazzi, or a guy group that had five to six boys included. He was given the opportunity to participate in honors' chorus and attend a large group chorus concert at a local women's college where he had to spend the weekend, so I chaperoned it, and Brady got to room with his good buddy Arjit. I saw Brady could escape through his singing. His voice was fine, and his speech was back, so why not use it? He seemed to enjoy singing, and he didn't mind doing it in front of large crowds. Although he was usually part of a larger group, he still didn't mind. There was one person that did though. One concert we attended, a young lady's knees locked, and she tumbled off the back of the bleachers being used as the platform. She was okay and had no injuries. The typical crowd was several hundred people, I am guessing. So yeah, it could be intimidating if someone didn't like standing in front of people with the attention on them. At the Orlando Supercross, Brady and I spoke in front of over fifty thousand people and had our faces on the large screens at each end of the stadium, so I felt sorry for the young girl.

When Brady was thirteen, we were introduced to hyperbaric oxygen therapy by someone in Denver. He had connections with a doctor in Atlanta. We took Brady to meet with the doctor to see if he thought the hyperbaric would be beneficial. His office was about eight miles further than where I worked, so it was a very long way from home. We were only able to continue these appointments for a short time. We eventually agreed to put one in our house so Brady could use it any time and as much as he wanted. He used it quite a bit over the months. I got in there several times myself. They are small, but I believe there are some positives with using them. The purpose of the chamber is to get as much extra oxygen as the body could absorb, which helps the brain with blood flow. There are many success stories online using this therapy. There are some professional athletes who have them and use them to rehab from an injury. After using a chamber for about six months, Brady was showing great improvements with his learning and memory. The same year, he passed all sections of the CRCT (criterion-referenced competency tests), so the proof was right in front of us.

One reason why we decided to try the chamber treatments was because the outpatient rehab center released Brady from any further rehab in January 2008. They cited the reason as not seeing enough improvement to keep going. The day I heard that was tough. I knew it would come, and it had after more than 2 years since his stroke. He wasn't close to 100 percent, which was the original target. It was a rough time trying to accept what we heard. Two and half years and he was not getting any better. He still had severe right-sided weakness with very little movement in the arm and leg. He had been doing rehab for a very long time. What do we know? Since the chamber came our way, we wanted to give it a shot. It gave Brady and us hope, but insurance didn't cover the cost for treatments, and money wasn't just falling out of the sky, so we had to be very picky about how many visits he could get and we could afford.

Other than the chamber, we tried a personal trainer for a short time. Any time someone showed signs of wanting to help or if we met someone who might be able to give me hope for Brady, I wanted to try them. Will began playing football and wrestling. His wrestling coach is the trainer we hired to work with Brady. Brady did the things he asked, and he worked hard. There are a lot of good things that can come from good exercise. Again, I was seeing signs of improvement in just only a handful of sessions with the trainer. Of course, this came with more complications; Brady himself this time. Brady was growing, getting older, and reaching puberty, and he started to see the years ticking off from his stroke date. About this time, I saw him give up and lose all hope for a sustainable and lasting recovery. We had recently found a church home with Brown's Bridge Community Church, a campus of North Point Ministries and Andy Stanley. Beth and I connected with the church, and we knew many people who also attended there. We got the boys involved with kids and groups their age, but Brady never took to the whole church thing. I felt like his main roadblock was his anger toward life and God about what happened to him. We continued to attend church on and off and became more regular attendees, eventually joining. Brady had several opportunities to attend weekend retreats and other social function, but he never wanted to go. This broke my heart because I knew God was the only way he would find peace and healing. Will thoroughly enjoyed his group. He knew many kids attending there through football or school. He still enjoys going today. He has attended several Walking Wisely weekends as well as a few other functions.

To this day, I have never asked Will to open up about his feelings regarding his brother's situation. He has helped Brady adapt and had to become the big brother at such an early age. It took all three of us to care for Brady at times.

How do you ask a five- or seven-year-old to help? He has never questioned it and jumped right in with both feet.

The three years of middle school was good to Brady. He continued to grow with friends and his confidence. He made the middle school play in eighth grade too. He actually put himself out there and was included in the play as a skateboard dude. He had some speaking parts and attempted the group dancing. When I saw the play the first time, I was so proud of him. As with any child becoming a young adult, the transitions from middle school to high school can be scary. I hear of how scared they are about it all the time from friends who have kids younger than Brady,. Fear! I have lived in fear ever since June 10, 2005. I have worried every school year, every event, every time he slept over at a friend's house. One of the most heartfelt things I have witnessed is his friends' embrace of him. Every one of his friends has helped him tie his shoes, carry something, fix his meal, and many other kind things. It makes me feel so blessed to have people like Doster, Arjit, Devon, Jonathan, and many others in his life. Not only have the young men been young men of God, but Brady has had several girl friends who continued to show him he is no different than them.

As we prepared for his transition to high school, I would not be given the same platform as I was with the other schools. At the high school level, they really wanted Brady being his own self advocate and taking ownership of what his needs are rather than relying on Mom and Dad. I had the hardest time letting go of this because I had always been there for him and in control of it. Every January, Brady has an annual meeting to go over his IEP. This is a time we can modify it if necessary, whether we are adding items or taking something off. At the high school level, Brady has to attend those meetings. He didn't embrace this like he should at first, but he did connect with Coach T, his caseworker at school. Coach T taught Brady how to be a self-advocate. I learned to rely on Coach T for his guidance and education of what I needed to do and not do. The high school Brady attends is pretty big. He goes to school with kids who look like grown adults. Some of the athletes make Brady look like Tiny Tim. As I write this, Brady is six feet tall, so he isn't the shortest kid.

> Trust in the Lord with all your heart and lean not on your own understanding; in all your ways acknowledge him, and he will make your paths straight.
>
> Proverbs 3:5–6 (NIV)

Why didn't I read this before? Why didn't I know this during this transition time? I could have found peace in this scripture.

Brady's freshman year was a learning curve for him and me. He was navigating a new school with new kids and new beginnings, while I was dealing with letting go of my little boy. All of us have a hard time letting go at times, but this was especially hard for me, considering the circumstances. After spending three years in middle school in chorus, Brady decided he didn't want to do it anymore. I still don't know why other than he wasn't thrilled about the type of music they sing. He likes current pop, country, and contemporary Christian music and more. He chose to take broadcasting, which was neat for him. Though he had issues with handling the camera, he did fine with being on camera and voice over type assignments. He struggled with French, but I did too. I took four years and traveled abroad and still struggled with it. Oddly enough, when Brady asked me for help, most of what I learned came back to me quickly. I took French about twenty-three years ago, so recalling something I hadn't used in a long time was crazy. I think the Arjit's transfer to another school might have also played a part in Brady's choice to not pursue chorus. Arjit and Brady were in chorus together, and I believe Arjit was a safety net for Brady when it came to being in a group like that and standing in front of all the eyes watching.

Brady began meeting girls and started asking several out on dates. He asked one girl to homecoming, and she accepted his offer. He was excited. This meant we had to head to the mall to find something to wear. Brady didn't own anything homecoming worthy. We got him a tie, button-down shirt, and some black slacks. He looked sharp. He had known this girl for any years, and they were in chorus together. They would text, but when he got around her, it's like he just froze up. Part of this was due to his age and the other was his lack of confidence. I don't think he expected the date would be such a success, but it was and good for him, a confidence booster. When he got home, he told me all the things they did and how the night went for him. They remain friends today. It shows Brady he doesn't have to be the boyfriend all the time to have great people in his life. He attended several football games with friends, and we continued to allow room for growth by letting him go with friends on the weekends, such as going to the movies and other activities some might find silly, but giving him the chance to grow up was needed. His acceptance of his situation grew more with each year, but it also grew more frustrating. I warned him at some point he would hit a wall with it and want more results. I wasn't ready to accept it myself, but he wasn't either. There were several times during his first two years of high school where he would come home frustrated and mad, even crying. He wanted to be like the other kids. The funny thing is everyone who knew him thought of him as normal, like everybody else. He was one of the guys. They didn't care if he couldn't play sports or had to think of safety first, but Brady did. It is very hard for people to see the big picture when we are in the picture. Brady needed to step back and realize he was just like the others. He attended the general classes like everyone else, and he was meeting his IEP goals set in the past. At the last annual IEP meeting, he was able to remove some accommodations, which is a great accomplishment.

During the sophomore year, Brady had to take driver's education. Wait a minute. He was getting ready to drive. Oh no, the time is here. Beth and I asked ourselves in years past if Brady would ever drive. Now all the sudden, the time was hitting us in the face. On one hand, I was excited, but on the other, I was freaking out. I know Beth was freaking out because she told me she wasn't ready for this, so I had to teach him. I suck at driving. I can't teach him. The class was different than I expected. He was taught in a simulator with the turn signals on the floor and had to be activated by pressing your foot on a button. What cars are made like this? This proved to be a major problem for Brady because he couldn't press the brake pedal and the turn signal button with the same foot, so he crashed a lot. He did well, I guess, considering he was awarded a certificate. During the class, he also had to take a mandated drug and alcohol course. This is required in order to get you licensed in Georgia. He was getting very excited about driving, and his parents were getting scared like the rest of the parents with kids that age. Cool thing about Brady was he never had to use special instruments inside the car. I taught him how to use his left foot for the pedals instead of the right one like me. He moved his right foot out of the way, and off he went driving the car. He turned fifteen, and I thought for sure we would be headed for the DMV (department of motor vehicles), but nope. Brady didn't show any interest in driving at first, and I believe it was because he wasn't sure he could do it. I didn't want to push him at first, but the days turned into weeks and then months. I started trying to encourage him a little. I knew I needed to teach him and get his confidence up so he could see this was going to be fine. He needed to drive however it looked; this was part of growing up. I finally downloaded the driver's manual and put it on his bed, giving him the hint it was time. Finally, one day before he turned sixteen, he wanted to take the written section of the test to get his learner's permit. He read the book, and we went to the DMV for the test. We walked up to the counter and turned in the stacks of paperwork they requested. He went to the computer room and took his test. When he came out, I knew something was wrong; he had failed it. He passed the first section but not the second, so he would have to go back later. I tried to explain to him that not everyone passes. When we were leaving, there were other kids failing it also. I took him to school and waited until the next morning to take him back to the testing center. We made the trip back to the center, and this time, he aced part 2, so a permit would be landing in his wallet.

The summer started with Brady being very interested in driving when he could, but he got sick for about two weeks and lost all motivation. By this time, it was time to start his sophomore year. The year started like all the others, lots of school supplies to buy and paperworks. Both kids were excited to see their friends because after all, that's all school is for, right? The year progressed and then homecoming came around again. Was Brady asking someone out this year? Brady and his friends decided to meet at the school this year and hang out in a group rather than go with dates. However, the night would end much different than the previous year. The year before, he came home filled with so much joy, plus he went with a date. I picked him up from the school, and he wouldn't say much, so I knew something happened or his mind was on something important. When we pulled up to the house, he let go with, "I am tired of this, and I want it to go away. I am tired of being different. I want to be normal," in a sad voice with tear-filled eyes. My heart sank. I poked around with him to see if something had happened at the dance, but he denied it and assured me nothing happened; it was him and his feelings. I wasn't really prepared for this. I did my best to console him. We even went to McDonalds in the middle of the night. I knew deep down I couldn't change him, his views, or his condition. Then he went to bed, and the next day, things seemed okay. The only thing I kept telling him was that he has to work hard to change things. They don't change themselves. He has hit this point several times since that night. He continues to search for a magic pill or magical surgery to repair the damage, but it doesn't exist.

Sharing Me

I get scared sometimes when I think about my kids. My children who I have wiped tears, applied Band-Aids, kissed good-night, and attempted to keep safe from negative influences will soon be young adults. Brady was there. Have you ever thought what this looks like? I have so many times.

As I write about this journey I have witnessed, I have shown ways on how Brady has grown over the last eight years. He has done really well becoming the young person I hoped him to be. He can do many things on his own, which is great and will provide him more confidence as he completes high school and look toward college.

After Brady's stroke, I wondered what milestones he would achieve and which ones he might never get to. In the early stages of his recovery, I didn't second-guess the doctors on their full recovery speech, but I did doubt to what extent they meant. Brady has come so far. It excites me to tell people about him and explain the depth of challenges he has faced and overcome. A nine-year-old boy who couldn't walk, cry, speak, write, or think has transformed into a great-looking young man who now walks, cries, speaks, writes left-handed, and has his own thoughts.

My first milestone for Brady was to have him attend a normal school with normal classes and normal homework. He achieved that very quickly. The brain was always my biggest concern, so seeing him doing great things in school meant he was getting better. Sure, the physical challenges were and continue to be hard to overlook. Brady worked very hard in his rehab so he could get better every time. In 2008, when the therapists told us there was nothing left to do with him and he would need to prepare himself to learn how to compensate with the results, it was hard for me. I harp on this because of the simple things we take for granted. Earlier, I challenged everyone to get up one day and only use one word to communicate. No one probably did it; I didn't expect them to. Here is another simple task Brady can't do—try tying shoes with only one hand. I am sure it can be done, but we haven't been able to teach him or master it. What does Brady do about his shoes? We tie them, or he wears shoes where ties stay intact then slips his shoes on. If a shoe comes untied while at school or something, he has to rely on his friends or teachers. It may seem petty to let something like this bother me, but how many times do we tie our shoes per day? A lot. Ever thought what it would be like if you couldn't open a jar or bottle of water the first time you bring them home? What about while in school, trying to carry all those heavy books and open a door? Thank goodness for backpacks; those have been a blessing. How about personal hygiene like cutting your fingernails or shaving? These are two things Brady struggles with every week now. How do you hold a can of shaving cream and squirt it out with the same hand? That part can be done, but what hand do you put the shaving cream in when the other hand is drawn up to your shoulder and in a closed fist? His brother, mother, and I have to cut his fingernails. Okay, so what? When he leaves our nest, then what does he do? How does he cut his own nails? Three of the four limbs not too bad, but what about the left hand, the only one he has that functions?

All of these things, and there many more, are simple life tasks that he struggles with every day. Strokes are so powerful and change a life forever. When Brady was younger, he liked some of Hilary Duff's music. While Brady was in the hospital, I would listen to her as a remembrance of things he liked before the stroke. We would play her music and others to see if he would respond to them. One day, I was listening to one of her CDs and a song really hit me. Although the lyrics probably had a different meaning considering the title of the song is "Who's That Girl," as I listened to them, the song hit home about what Brady had to be feeling. Think about it for a minute. One second you are the person you are right now, then the next second, you are feeling like someone else, life changed, something went wrong.

The song asks the question about who someone is and that can't be the person you want. It goes on to ask the question of who is the person running my life and even stating that everything is same but then again, everything is different. As Brady lay in bed, struggling to be the person he once was, he was different. He would say, "I just want to be normal and like I was!" As I listened to that song over and over again, I could only hope he would find himself, find the new Brady.

We would tell him all the time he is the same Brady with the same personality but he was changed. He struggled to be social now that he walked with a limp and his right arm would just hang there with little use. I would encourage you to search for the lyrics on the Internet and read them to understand the magnitude and power they have when you put them in the context of Brady's situation or anyone suffering like him.

The same can be said when we lose a loved one. I regret moving away from God during these hard times because there is so much more peace with him.

> So do not fear, for I am with you; do not be dismayed, for I am your God. I will strengthen you and help you; I will uphold you with my righteous right hand.
>
> Isaiah 41:10 (NIV)

> "Come to me, all you who are weary and burdened, and I will give rest. Take my yoke upon you and learn from me, for I am gentle and humble in heart, and you will find rest for you souls. For my yoke is easy and my burden is light."
>
> Matthew 11:28–30 (NIV)

These are two recent verses where I have found peace with not only Brady's situation but anytime I find myself forgetting God is mighty and can handle all, which I can't.

For Christmas 2012, we gave Brady an opportunity to get involved with something he enjoyed. We signed him up with a music and voice coach so he would be involved in something other than video games. He attended for several months and made two recordings, which I like. Now I am not a music producer or expert of the craft, but at least they were easy on the ears. I would love to see him doing something with his voice. The gaming thing is cool and all, but there will be a time when he will need to have career in something, and using his voice would be a great path for him. However, maybe something in the gaming industry could be good. After all, he plays all his games one-handed and whoops people all the time. This is another milestone he reached. He taught himself how to play Xbox and PlayStation one-handed without any help. He was not going to be denied the fun of video games. Since he was two, he always had to have some gadget in his hand. It reminds me of my father-in-law, Larry. Will got Larry's look, and Brady got his love for electronics. Thanks, Dad.

It was close to seven or eight months before he became interested driving again. He got his permit. I am not sure if this was like most other teenagers or not. I didn't read much into it. All of the sudden, he got up one day and said, "I want to get my license now." We had a lot to do before he could get his license though. We had to log the forty hours with six of those being at night. He needed to improve overall, and I still had a lot to teach him. In June of 2013, Brady achieved the feat of obtaining his license. He became a full-time driver. Another milestone hit! There are other small things he has done, and there are larger things he does that continue to put me in awe of him. Here is a kid who can do ten one-arm pull-ups. He may not be able to do pushups because of the limitations, but a chin-up and pull-up is another thing. I don't know too many people who can do those. But above all the physical things he can do now, the one thing I am most proud of is he has finally started to lean on God for support and guidance.

> It's hard for a family member to be stuck in the hospital or even a family member that had cancer or even has cancer. They just got to keep their head up! Because in the end everything is going to be okay. And they have to have a positive attitude because at the end of the battle what you going through it's going to be okay. You just got to keep you head up and not let it fall and push through the day being strong.
>
> —Brady Jones, February 19, 2013

Well this really good friend told me something that I will remember for life. She said I am a survivor, I am an unmormal 16 year old boy with a future out there. If some people don't know, I had a stroke when I was 9. It's been a very long time when I was that age and now I am 16 heading to be 17. When I had my stroke, my family was heartbroken but God pulled us back up and restored us and now we have great people out there caring for us. Thanks Arjit Saxena, Devon Black, Brad Barco, Jonathan Meakin, Sarah Nettuno, Taylor Butterfield, Tommy Jones, Will Jones, Brad Phillips.

—Brady Jones, April 28, 2013

Hello Facebook. Well here it goes. I have been through a lot and my family. I was 9 years old when I had my stroke. My whole right side was paralyzed and now I am 17, that's 8 years ago. Back then I was stuck in a hospital. It seems like a century. I remember when I was in a wheel chair and then I got fed up with it and with all my strength I got up and on my two feet was walking. There is a limp but still I was walking and speech was a little harder but I managed to speak again but done with my past. That was so long ago and just forget the past, please do because man, you got a future out there. I am 17 now and have my license and that was no problem and in my junior year of high school. I even managed to play Xbox 360 with one hand. My friends say that's insane but that how I adapted. I have great friends and a wonderful family. Love you guys. I couldn't ask for anything more than God because I got it already and thanks dad and mom for everything and Will (ended with a picture with this saying) – When you're down to nothing, God is up to something. The faithful see the invisible, believe the incredible and then receive the impossible.

—Brady Jones, July 19, 2013

Brady, you're a good friend of mine and all I have to say is that you're a brave man. Faith is the way to go because with God, anything is possible.

—Posted on Brady Jones's Facebook
by a friend on July 20, 2013.

There is no other way to end this thought except by holding a tissue.

Brady mentioned there are people who care, and he is right. He has met some great people who have shown him there is more out there. Not only his everyday friend, but the Supercross rider and a football player have come into his life at various times, not to mention the great doctors who he still sees from time to time. About two years ago, I met a trainer who knew someone who might be good for Brady to meet. One night, Will, Brady, and I met the trainer at California Pizza Kitchen near North Point Mall. There we had the privilege to meet Brandon Lynch, a former Colt and Canadian champion. I even held his championship ring. I am not sure how he wears the overly sized and heavy thing. Brandon wanted to know Brady a little, and by the end of the night, they were exchanging phone numbers. Brandon told him to call or text him any time. Did he mean it though? These guys meet people all the time, and this couldn't be happening. Years have passed, and Brandon is now with an NFL team in a coaching position, but one thing has never failed, he has always been there for Brady, and even me. I find myself texting him more than Brady at times, not because he is a pro athlete, but as a strong God-fearing person, he lifts me up. The other night, I sent him a text about something Will did, and we chatted for about ten minutes. I also texted him when Brady did something good or was down, and Brandon always has the right things to say. He was brought in our lives by God, and God speaks through him. Thanks, buddy.

Learning to Cope:
What to Do

How do I cope? Where do I turn? I turned to myself for so many years. I dove into my work and career to become the best I could at what I do—design homes and lead others. Early on, I dove into my riding and would make excuses for needing to be away or even busy. Eventually, I would grow into a position with the national homebuilder, which put me in a position to be on the road almost weekly. At first, I thought this was cool and I would meet some great people. Little did I realize it put my family in turmoil. My wife and kids had to figure out how to live without me most of the time. There were some weeks where I was gone from Monday until Thursday. *No big deal*, I thought. *There are plenty of fathers who do this.* Husbands travel all the time. I guess everyone has their own story to tell and problems, but I didn't realize I shut my eyes on Brady's situation or on anything else going on at home. When I was at home, I was usually staying busy, playing on my iPad or playing golf because I need a break from the long week.

We all cope differently, but what I realized was what I was doing wasn't coping; I was running. Sure, I put on a front and could be the person I needed to be when I needed to be, but on the inside, I was dying. This didn't get any better as the years went on; it got worse. I would tell Beth and the kids, "Daddy has been gone all week, so I am going to play golf to relax." Sure? Oh, I did play golf, but why did I need other outlets to relax and why not spend good family time at home? Why wasn't I being fulfilled? This was about the time I found my way back to Christ.

We had some friends who asked us to join a small group through our church. I was very hesitant at first, but we did it. It lasted for several years, and along the way, Beth was able to talk about her feelings, and I grew my faith once again. Though we aren't part of the small group anymore, we did find peace in the fellowship with the group. It was also shortly after that I began to fall back into my old ways of doing things my way and not God's way. Why couldn't I rely on God? When I did rely on him and surrendered my troubles over to him, he has always been there and worked out the situation as he planned. Why doubt? I don't have the answer to that question. I wish I knew because I could have had peace years ago and found ways to help Beth with her grieving. Beth began a Bible study and was able to meet a group of ladies who led her to facing her grief and also led her to the Bible in a more spiritual way than ever before. I witnessed God working through her. Believe it or not, he was working through her for me too. Once again, I started reading a daily devotional and the Word of God. I am not a good reader as I am more of a doer and need to see things being done. God must know this because he led me to write this book as a way for me to find continued peace and to share my story with others. When I was in doubt, he was there with me every time. He spoke to me, and I missed it over the years because I was still hurting. I closed my heart from him, but it's because of Christ that I found peace. When I turned forty in 2012, I designed a tattoo with the help of others and had it placed on the inside of my left bicep. People thought I was crazy, but I wanted something permanent to remind me of where I have been and who always save me. It also serves as my conversation starter with some people. When I chose the artist to do the tattoo, he told me what to expect; others even told me it would hurt pretty bad since it was going to be on a tender place. When I laid on the table, there was no pain. There was no more doubting. There was no more walking away. I never even flinched. I never asked why. I knew because I was at peace. The image is a cross made of nails with the crown of thorns Jesus wore when he died, died for me.

I started writing this book about three or four years ago. I wrote several chapters and would delete them and write more. Finally, after about four chapters, I stopped. I walked away. This was about the same time I walked away from God in a way. I wanted to do the book to cope, to get my feelings out, to share the story, to share the pain, to share the trying times, not only what Brady went through but also what I went through. I continued walking on my own and left the book to sit. I took another promotion at work, and this time, I would be the head of architecture nationally. Wow, what an honor and what a position! I was fulfilled for a while. I was doing what I loved to do and making things happen. I got to call the shots for my department, and I had control of the product designs, but I still found myself wanting more. I needed more. In December of 2012, there was another position open, and I thought to myself, *This would give me even more responsibility, and I would be viewed as more successful. I should talk to them about letting me run both departments.* Okay, I must have thought I could concur the world or something. On December 21, I remember sitting in my office and speaking to my boss about this bonehead idea I had. He asked me, "Why do you care what price we pay for lumber? What gets you going is by putting your thumbprint on the front door of all the homes." I really didn't look to this person as a God, but was God speaking to me again through this person? I struggle to see it sometimes; however, he was right, and I heard it loud and clear. I didn't need to take on more. I actually needed to do less but better with my time. I continued to think about this conversation for months.

On January 18, 2013, Beth's fortieth birthday, we found out I had a melanoma. I knew nothing about skin cancer, but I did know this wasn't good. The phone call scared me to death. I thought I would die within three months. I was never afraid of dying, but I was afraid of leaving my family, especially Brady. How would he cope? We dealt with the prognosis the best we could and sought medical advice. We found a great doctor who performed surgery on me on Valentine's Day to remove the cancer and test my lymph nodes to insure the cancer hasn't spread. My recovery was terrible. Having an incision in my armpit and a six-inch incision down my back wasn't fun at all. I thought for sure I would be back at work in no time. My new boss had put a little pressure on me, so I knew I needed to get back. Against my wife's wishes, I returned to work as I originally planned, but I couldn't drive or lift anything over five pounds. After a few weeks, I was back to driving and had the clearance to travel for work. I told myself, "This is God telling me to slow down." I needed to rely on others to do more, and I needed to focus on getting better and on my family. This hit Brady really hard. I remember praying to God to just heal me but more importantly, guide Brady in understanding. I continued with my recovery and at the same time, continued reading God's Word to find peace.

On my three-month checkup, I was still looking good and had no signs of cancer. My doctor told me I was clean for now, but he wouldn't say I am cancer-free. My body wants to create the cells for some reason, so I have to be very careful with the sun. Also, I left my job on May 10 for various reasons. What was I going to do? Now, I have no job or income. How would I provide for the family? All these questions are common when someone goes through something like this. I prayed for God to give me guidance to his path and his will. In the succeeding weeks, he showed up about a hundred times. I decided to start my own design firm located in Atlanta. With my national exposure, I had the experience most didn't, so I could provide services across the country. I began networking to people, from builders to marketing firms as well as mentors and past leaders. In front of me was God's plan—open my own firm. Well, not quite. Yes, opening the firm was a positive thing, but it helped me to see God's plan. I was working out of our house with a flexible schedule and time to focus on my family. I took the kids to school on the last several weeks of school, took Brady to get his license, and occasionally took my bride to breakfast or lunch. Even better than doing those things, I got a new daily devotional. Every morning, I now spend time with God in my office. For the first in a very long time, I feel joy. I feel hope. I feel fulfilled. It could be because I work for myself, but that isn't it at all. It could be work has been busy, so financially, things look good right now. No, that isn't it. What is it? I have finally put God first in my life, and he is the reason I moved past the coping to a life of fulfillment. Did God lead me down these roads? Probably. Did he want me to hurt? Not likely. He wants his children to rely on him always just as how we want our kids to rely on us. God loves us as a parent loves their child.

> I have been crucified with Christ and I no longer live, but Christ lives in me. The life I live in the body, I live by faith in the Son of God, who loved me and gave himself for me.

> Galatians 2:20 (NIV)

Not only has God led me to spend more time with my family, whom I had been neglecting, but he gave me the time to share what he has done for me through this book. I struggled over the last few years to find time, but now I have the time outside of meeting my clients' deadlines. I can work when I need to. I can take time off when I see fit.

While on a recent business trip to Denver, I met with Mike, an ex-employer, one afternoon to discuss books and how to get something published. Mike had written two books, with one already published, and the second one was close to being completed. He explained to me the processes he followed as well as a few pointers. I needed to decide which option to take and start the process. I made some mental notes from my meeting with Mike and thanked him for his time that afternoon. It wasn't until several weeks later when I decided to finally start researching what I needed to do using Mike's guidance. Beth was in my office with me one evening. We were trying to teach each other how to set up the company accounting structure. Afterward, she remained on my computer, so I decided to use our laptop to cruise the internet. I searched *publishing* and *book publishing* to see what I could find. One of the very first search results was Tate Publishing, so I clicked the link.

What took place over the next four, or maybe five days, was clearly God's work being done. I received an e-mail from someone interested in my book, but, wait, the book wasn't finished yet. We traded e-mails for a few days. Soon thereafter, I received a contract, offering me the chance to write my book, share my story, spread pediatric stroke awareness, and testify how the glory of God worked in me to get me here. This project was going to happen, but now it was up to me to get my rear in gear to complete the book.

I had some questions regarding the contract, so we set a time to visit via phone to discuss the process further. We discussed what it meant to be a writer, possibly doing book signings and many other things, including how we felt we were brought together. Shortly after hanging up with her, I executed the agreement, paid my publicist fee, and done. I became a writer and needed to finish my book. My eyes were truly opened by God—his promise, his love, his grace, his timing, and his plan for me.

I am reminded that there are people living like I was, and when I hear the following lyrics, I think, *What if my story, our story, could reach one person, maybe two, maybe a family, maybe two? Would it help them?* I pray for each person living with pain, and I pray this book and my story will help someone out there or someone they know to heal, cope, and find their way back to God, or even for the first time.

> Give me Your eyes for just one second
> Give me Your eyes so I can see
> Everything that I keep missing
> Give me Your love for humanity
> Give me Your arms for the broken-hearted
> The ones that are far beyond my reach
> Give me Your heart for the ones forgotten
> Give me Your eyes so I can see
> Yeah
>
> —Brandon Heath and Jason Ingram,
> "Give Me Your Eyes," What If We, (2008)

GIVE ME YOUR EYES

Written by: Brandon Heath and Jason Ingram

© 2008 Sony/ATV Music Publishing LLC, Sitka 6 Music, and publisher(s) unknown. All rights on behalf of Sony/ATV Music Publishing

LLC and Sitka 6 Music administered by Sony/ATV Music Publishing LLC, 8 Music Square West, Nashville, TN 37203. All rights reserved. Used by permission.

GIVE ME YOUR EYES

Written by Jason Ingram & Brandon Heath

© 2008 by Perrtunes, Ltd and Windsor Way Music Peertunes, Ltd administers on behalf of itself and Windsor Way Music.

Used by permission.

All Rights Reserved.

Faith

A s I bring this book and story to a close, "God of Wonders" is playing on my computer. It is 5:42 a.m., and I have been up all night, proofing and putting the finishing touches on the book, so it can be presented to you. I am very excited that the journey will soon be out for all to see and read. There are many people living in pain due to many different issues. Whether you are facing a family member's death, a friend's death, troubled marriage, family member hooked on drugs or alcohol, or an illness, find peace in knowing there is a God and he is there to help you and me.

If you are struggling or fighting to overcome, lean on Jesus Christ, and he will provide the path, the peace, and the light. The dictionary defines faith as a strong belief in a supernatural power or powers that control human destiny. The Bible defines faith as "being sure of what we hope for and certain of what we do not see" (Hebrews 11:1).

I pray that you may be active in sharing your faith, so that you will have a full understanding of every good thing we have in Christ.

> Philemon 1:6–7 (NIV)

He replied, "Because you have so little faith. I will tell you the truth, if you have faith as small as a mustard seed, you can say to this mountain, "Move from here to there." and it will move. Nothing will be impossible for you."

> Matthew 17:20–21 (NIV)

To me, faith is trust. If I have faith in the Lord, then I must trust in the Lord. If I trust in the Lord, then I must have faith he will come through at the perfect time. As you read my story, I didn't always have this kind of faith or trust in God. It has taken me fighting through Brady's pain, my wife's pain, our depression, and even a bout with cancer. Now I have always known God was there for me, but I didn't always take him up on his offer to comfort me because I didn't trust him. Trusting God meant I wasn't in control.

Those who know your name will trust in you, for you, Lord, have never forsaken those who seek you.

> Psalm 9:10 (NIV)

When I am afraid, I will trust in you.

> Psalm 56:3 (NIV)

My closing prayer

Dear Heavenly Father, Lord Jesus, I praise your name and speak to you. You are the Way, the Path, the Light, the Healer, the Spirit, and Savior. Lord, only you know those in troubled times. You know their circumstance and understand their pain and sorrow. I pray you will grant them peace and strength. Please lay your hand on their shoulder and comfort them during this time of pain. I pray you will lead them to surrender it all to you. I pray they will trust in you, have faith in you. For the lost ones, I ask you to continue opening doors for them and showing them your way. Please grant them the eyes to see the open doors before you have to show them. Continue showing us your mercy and grace. I ask all these things in your glory, amen.

God Bless and thanks for allowing me to share our family, my thoughts, and my story with you.

Afterword

Eight years ago, when I was nine, I had the stroke this book describes. I couldn't walk or talk. It was like I was a giant baby. Yeah, I still remember that tragic day like it was yesterday, but I can't get bogged down. I have to pick my head up and move forward in life. I still remember when I was in a wheelchair and getting fed up, so I got myself up and started walking by the grace of God. My speech got better each week, but that was then. I am seventeen years old now with a super amazing family and great friends who have helped me through the thick and thin of my recovery. Who would have thought I would be driving, but guess what? I am. My next challenge is to prepare for college somewhere.

I have an awesome life and believe I am stronger now more than ever. It is with Christ in which we find strength to move forward, to face what comes our way. To my family and friends, I love you guys!

When you find yourself facing tough times, remember me and others like me who have powered through the adversity to find strength inside. Find the physical strength, trust in God, and call on your family and friends, and you too will "get up and walk again."

Thank you for allowing my dad to share about his view and my story.

—Brady Jones, July 2013

About the Author

Tommy Jones is the owner of Gordon / Thomas Design Group, LLC in Atlanta, Georgia, where he manages the firm and enjoys spending time with his family. He has over twenty-one years of experience in home design and has developed products all over the US. He has plenty to be proud of within his architectural career, from designing houses over 10,000 square feet to working with some amazing people along the way. But he has only been a writer for a year; however, don't let that stop you from reading his book.

Tommy has a love for the game of golf and mentoring others. Even though his golf game could always use some help, he finds comfort in helping cultivate younger ones in his field or any industry.

Mr. Jones has plenty of passion on the topic of healing a damaged and lost soul, considering he lived through some pretty rough days. His words are filled with emotion, which will move you at every turn. He has written his journey in a way you are able to connect and feel like you are right there beside him. He invites you to walk with him, cry with him, and become a stronger person.